Snowboarding

To

Nirvana

Also by the Author

FREDERICK LENZ

Snowboarding to Nirvana

St. Martin's Griffin

New York

Design by Jennifer Ann Daddio

Library of Congress Cataloging-in-Publication Data

Lenz, Frederick.
    Snowboarding to nirvana : a novel / Frederick Lenz.
        p.   cm.
    ISBN 0-312-18179-5
    I. Title.
PS3562.E496S65   1997
813'.54—dc2I   96-45535
                                                                        CIP

First St. Martin's Griffin Edition: January 1998

10   9   8   7   6   5   4   3   2   I

For Vayu

Acknowledgments

I would like to thank my agent, Nicholas Ellison, for his initial belief in the *Surfing the Himalayas* trilogy; my editor at St. Martin's Press, James Fitzgerald, for his continued support and good sense of humor; Louis Simpson, Ph.D., who taught me that critical method and poetry are not at odds with each other; Vayu the dog, my constant companion, to whom this book is dedicated; Master Fwap, the Oracle of Nepal, and all of the extraordinary Buddhist, Hindu, and Taoist masters I have had the opportunity to study with.

In addition I would like to thank my martial arts and scuba diving instructors for teaching me the Tao of high-performance athletics, and all of the other wonderful teachers I have had throughout the course of my life who have opened the doorways for me to the worlds of music, higher mathematics, computer science, and a myriad of other subjects.

I was in one of the most beautiful places in all the world, the Himalayan mountains. Several months before, in my endless quest for perfect snow, I had left my home in America and traveled by plane to Nepal with my two snowboards, to have the ultimate experience in snowboarding.

Shortly after arriving in Nepal, I was fortuitously met and befriended by an aged Tibetan Buddhist monk, a Master Fwap Sam-Dup, of the Rae Chorze-Fwaz Order of Tantric Buddhist Enlightenment. After an initial encounter and further conversations with Master Fwap, I spent several months traveling through the Himalayas with him, visiting Buddhist monasteries and places of power.

During our first weeks of traveling together, Master Fwap explained some of the basic concepts of Tantric Buddhist yoga and showed me how to apply those concepts to my snowboarding. He also allowed me to witness him perform a number of what I can only describe as "miracles," which defied all the laws of physics that I had been taught in the American schools I had attended.

I have written about my initial travels and conversations with Master Fwap, which constituted my initiation into Buddhist yoga and the metaphysics of snowboarding, in my previous book, *Surfing the Himalayas*. In the following pages I describe the second cycle of Master Fwap's Tantric Buddhist teachings and also some of the more advanced snowboarding techniques that Master Fwap revealed to me, as we roamed deeper and deeper into the more remote areas of the Himalayas.

I have taken the liberty of transforming these accounts—even though they are based on real-life occurrences—into a work of fiction. In transforming my actual experiences into fiction and to make this book both more enjoyable and informative for you to read, I have in some instances altered time periods, shortened trekking experiences, and made other chronological and content changes.

—Rama-Frederick Lenz, Ph.D.

PART ONE

The Web of Life

I

OUT ON A PEAK!

It was late afternoon in the Himalayas. I was standing on top of a remote mountain peak in northern Nepal. As I watched from my sixteen-thousand-foot vantage point, the sun momentarily ducked behind a gray-and-white cloud mass that hovered directly over the crest of some jagged mountains to the west.

As if triggered by the sun's sudden disappearance, a freezing, icy mountain breeze from the north assaulted the front of my body. Hurriedly, I zipped up my Gore-Tex down ski parka, rapidly pulled its hood up and over the top of my head, tugged on its straps, and secured it, firm and snug, around my freezing face.

The cold, stinging wind continued to rise as the sun moved swiftly on its ever-westward course. As I watched in awe, the color of the sky began to change from a light Nepalese blue into a soft, pastel rose and lavender tinged with deep purple and white streaks.

Standing alone, on an unnamed snow- and ice-covered peak, watching the everlasting montage of colors that filled the skies above me, I wished silently that I could remain in the breathtaking beauty of that time and place forever. But the rapidly rising icy wind, combined with the plummeting temperature, gave me no choice but to snowboard immediately down the mountainside or freeze to death, alone, in the oncoming Himalayan night.

My jet-black snowboard lay on the ground several yards ahead of me. I was about to mount my board and begin to snowsurf down the mountain—when suddenly I had a strong feeling that someone was standing directly behind me.

I quickly gave a nervous glance over my shoulder, but to my surprise no one was there! I was completely alone, out on a peak, in the late-afternoon snow.

Laughing out loud at the absurdity of the idea that someone else might be out on that same remote Himalayan peak, I turned back and looked at my snowboard . . . and yet, the strange feeling that I was being watched persisted.

Just as I was about to mount my snowboard, I heard a strong male voice call out my name from behind me. My stomach knotted. Reflexively, I swiveled around on the heels of my snowboarding boots to see who was there.

Much to my dismay, there was no one behind me at all! I was still completely alone at sixteen thousand feet.

I immediately assumed that I must be seriously losing it. "Probably the altitude," I muttered to myself. I quickly mounted my snowboard, hoping to get off the peak before my altitude-generated hallucinations worsened.

As I snapped my snowboarding boots into their bindings, I heard the voice for a second time. "The dimensions! The dimensions! What has happened to the dimensions? They are all disappearing!" I heard the voice say, in what I can only describe as an emotionally charged lament.

Without bothering to look behind me for a third time, I quickly pushed off on my snowboard and began my run down the snow- and ice-covered mountainside.

I felt better when I started to carve in and out of the deep

Himalayan powder. I kept my turns tight and completely focused my mind on snowboarding, consciously pushing the sound of that plaintive voice out of my memory until I finished the end of my run on the granular snow at the bottom of the mountain.

Zen and the Art of
Snowboarding

After an exhilarating ride down the mountain on my snowboard, I reached the bottom of the slope where—much to my surprise—I found Master Fwap waiting for me. He had a huge grin on his face!

I carefully brought my snowboard to a halt a safe distance in front of him and shouted out in amazement, "Master Fwap, what are you doing here?"

"Why, I'm waiting for you, of course," he replied in a matter-of-fact tone.

I hopped off my snowboard, removed my goggles, and stared at him. I was speechless.

"You look well," he remarked with a soft chuckle. "How have you been getting on with your snowboarding project?"

Master Fwap was referring to an assignment he had given me when I had last seen him several weeks ago. At that time, he recommended that I evolve my snowboarding from a consumer sport into a Buddhist practice that he referred to as "mindfulness."

Master Fwap had told me that the Buddhist practice of mindfulness is perfectly suited to snowboarding, because it is a type of meditation that is accomplished while a person is physically active. The most critical part of mindfulness, he had carefully explained to me, is to be consciously aware—while snowboarding—that my snowboard and I were "one."

At the time I wasn't particularly interested in learning how to meditate at all, let alone while snowboarding down some of the most difficult and treacherous slopes in the world, but Master Fwap had convinced me to try his mindfulness technique by promising that it would radically improve my snowboarding.

"Okay, I guess," I sheepishly replied to his question. "To tell you the truth, Master Fwap, I haven't really practiced your technique very often. Most of the time when I'm snowboarding, I get so involved in what I am doing that I forget to visualize that I am the board."

"Do not be discouraged. It takes both time and practice to turn an activity like snowboarding into meditation. Be patient. No matter how difficult it may seem at first, keep visualizing that you and your snowboard are one and that you are both made of the same energy."

"But it's so hard!" I complained.

"It's only as hard as you think it is," Master Fwap quickly replied.

"Master Fwap, that's easy for you to say. You grew up here in the East. All of your cultural traditions support Buddhist yoga. Where I come from we have cultural traditions like television, Bud Lite, and football."

"You are feeling sorry for yourself and making excuses when none are necessary," he curtly replied. "Life is hard, harsh, and cruel; it is also incredibly beautiful and worthy of our deepest respect."

"Master Fwap, I don't understand what you mean by that. I know that life is simultaneously difficult and beautiful, but what does that have to do with what we were just talking about? You always say things like that just to change the subject."

7

"I am not changing the subject. I am just putting the subject into its proper perspective. We can't really talk about the practice of meditation, in either a physically active or passive form, unless we see it as an interactive mental and spiritual process that intimately connects us with the rest of the universe."

"But what does that have to do with the beauty and harshness of life? I simply get distracted by the difficulty of snowboarding down some of the slopes, that's all. I still don't understand what you're driving at."

"I'm not driving at anything," he quickly replied. "You are. I am simply standing at the foot of this beautiful mountain waiting for you to ask me the 'just right' question for the precise moment and location that we are in." He spoke in a melodious tone of voice. It was apparent from both the relaxed expression on his face and the tone of his voice that Master Fwap was not the least bit perplexed by my sudden emotional outburst.

"And what question might that be?" I asked. I had learned from my previous experiences with Master Fwap that he had a way of leading me into long and complex metaphysical conversations through which he attempted to teach me Buddhist yoga.

To be honest with you, at that exact moment in time and space, I was a young man who was not the least bit interested in learning anything more about Buddhist metaphysics. I was tired, hungry, and cold. I had definitely been weirded-out by my experiences with the strange voice back up on the peak. The only conscious thought in my mind then was to get into the local village a short distance away as soon as possible. I had made arrangements earlier in the day with a Nepalese family who lived in the village to spend the night in their home. I wanted to get there, eat some hot food, and crash. That's it.

But it was clear from Master Fwap's voice and from the playful gleam in his eyes that I wasn't going to get off that lightly. My previous experiences with Master Fwap had taught me that he was highly telepathic and had an uncanny ability to read minds. I knew that he was aware of my discomfort. However, as I contemplated Master Fwap's question, I had a feeling that I wasn't going to end up in the village with hot food and a soft sleeping bag in the very near future, if at all.

"You know all too well which question I am referring to," he continued, his broad smile gently accentuating the small wrinkles that lined his aged Tibetan face. "Close your eyes, clear your mind, silence your thoughts, and the question will come to you."

Following Master Fwap's instructions, I closed my eyes and attempted to quiet my thoughts. At first, thoughts buzzed through my mind like a swarm of angry bees, but after a few minutes of focusing on emptiness, my thoughts began to slow. Several more minutes passed, and instead of listening to my thoughts, I began to hear the wind rushing through the snowy mountain passes above us.

Then, quite suddenly, without knowing how I was so certain, I knew exactly what the "just right" question was. I opened my eyes and asked, "Whose voice was it that I heard up on top of the peak, Master Fwap?"

"I can't tell you that yet," Master Fwap replied, as a serious expression suddenly fell over his face. "Before I can determine that, please tell me what the voice said to you."

"It said something about the dimensions being missing. That's really all that I remember. The voice sounded very sad to me."

Master Fwap looked at me with a vacant expression. I had the strange feeling that he wasn't totally in his body right then.

Waiting for Master Fwap's answer, I studied his appearance. He was approximately five foot two, very thin, and couldn't have weighed more than one hundred and twenty-five pounds. From my six-foot-three-inch vantage point, I had a clear view of his neatly shaved, round head.

His face, like that of so many Tibetan people, was gently wrinkled from a lifetime of exposure to bright sunlight and the thin air at extremely high altitudes. Even though his skin was marked with many small, fine lines of age, it didn't seem old and worn. In fact, his skin had a healthy and youthful glow.

Master Fwap had told me once that he was seventy-three years old. His eyes were hazel colored, and they seemed to change hue according to his mood. When he smiled—which was frequently—he revealed a perfect set of pearly white teeth.

His saffron-colored monk's robe was ancient. In places, its color was uneven and faded from extended exposure to the sun. He wore small boots and high stockings. His English, while perfect, was slightly accented. While I stood shivering in the oncoming Himalayan night, dressed in America's warmest and best technology, Master Fwap, dressed in his light cotton robe, seemed oblivious to the freezing wind that was buffeting our bodies.

After several more minutes of silence, Master Fwap's expression sharpened. He then began to speak to me in a quiet, barely audible tone against the din of the rising mountain winds of sunset.

"There are many mysteries in the Himalayas," he slowly began. "There are many astral doorways and parallel dimensions hidden deep within the mountains here. These astral doorways and dimensions lead to thousands of different parallel universes. The spirits of great masters who left their bodies long ago occasionally return to this world to convey an important piece of information to someone here. They step in and out of these astral doorways to do so. Today, when you were up on the mountain, one of these disembodied masters came and spoke to you and gave you an important message—"

"You mean I wasn't simply hallucinating back up there on the peak?" I interrupted.

"No, you weren't."

"Well, Master Fwap, what did he mean? And why would a disembodied yoga master speak to me?"

"I can't tell you that."

"Wait a second. How could I hear him if he wasn't in his body? How could he speak to me without a voice?"

I was suddenly very suspicious. I thought that perhaps Master Fwap was just kidding me.

"He spoke to you telepathically," Master Fwap calmly replied. "You heard him talking inside of your mind."

"What dimensions was he talking about? Why can't you tell me what he meant? I thought that you were enlightened. Doesn't that mean you know everything?"

"So many questions. Yes, as you know, I am enlightened. But to be enlightened does not mean that you know all things."

"Well, then, what *does* it mean?"

I had asked him before what it was like to be enlightened, and he always seemed to give me contradictory answers. I had a feeling that his answer would by no means be short, so using my snowboard as a seat, I sat down and relaxed, preparing myself for what I assumed would be a long discourse.

"When you are enlightened, you live in a condition of perfect inner light and happiness. Enlightenment is the complete awareness of all things, without mental modifications. But that is not the same as knowing particular things. The knowledge of particular things in the occult dimensions is part of the *siddha* powers. Different masters have different *siddha* powers, but none of us has them all. I don't have access to the particular dimensions that you need to see into to understand the riddle that the disembodied master has given you to solve."

"Well, if *you* don't know, how will *I* ever find out?"

"I know someone, although I have not seen him for many years, who might be able to help you. It is a long journey, though, and he can be difficult...."

I shifted my position slightly on my snowboard and asked, "What do you mean by difficult, and why do you think that what I heard up on the peak is a riddle?"

At this point, I was becoming very perplexed by everything that Master Fwap was saying. I wanted a quick, easy, simple explanation.

"The master spoke to you because he saw that you needed his help. I cannot tell you what he meant, and even if I could, my explanation wouldn't help you. By solving his riddle you will solve yourself, if you know what I mean. I can tell you, however, that it is very unusual for a disembodied master to return to this plane and communicate with someone, as he did with you. I'm sure it is very important for you to solve the riddle of the missing dimensions. I hope for your sake that you solve it before you leave the Himalayas and return to America," Master Fwap said mysteriously.

As I listened to Master Fwap, I was beginning to get anxious. My previous experiences with him had convinced me that there was much more to life than met my eyes.

I had originally come to Nepal to snowboard the Himalayas. Since snowboarding has always been a transcendental as well as physical experience for me, when I initially "ran into" Master Fwap, I was open to some of his ideas about Buddhism, particularly when he demonstrated to me that there was a definite interrelationship between proficiency and advancement in Buddhism and advancement in snowboarding.

Initially I was skeptical that learning about Tantric Buddhism and practicing meditation would improve my ability to snowboard, but after traveling with Master Fwap for many weeks in the Himalayas, and learning and practicing the snowboarding and meditation techniques he recommended to me, I had discovered that he was absolutely right.

My previous physical and metaphysical experiences with him had been so powerful, and at the same time so practical, that I had made an internal decision that I was more than willing to follow him anywhere, so long as it would continue to help me to become a better snowboarder.

While I didn't really want to get involved with solving the riddle of the missing dimensions, suddenly I felt that I had to. I mustered my courage and asked Master Fwap a question that, without realizing it at the time, would take me on an adventure that would change my life forever.

"Who is the person you think might be able to help me understand all of this?"

"There is a certain Oracle who lives in the Thunderbolt Monastery. He has access to many of the more obscure dimensional planes. He might be able to assist you, but as I said, he can be quite difficult at times. . . ."

"What do you mean by that? In what way is he difficult?"

Master Fwap did not answer my question. Instead, he remained silent. Then after a brief time he spoke: "I think the best way to answer your question is for you to meet the Oracle yourself. Come with me to the Thunderbolt Monastery. You have done enough wboarding for now. It's time for you to resume your Buddhist education. The voice on the mountain was telling you something important. Come, we will inquire of the Oracle together!"

Without hesitation, Master Fwap turned and started walking down the snow-covered slope toward the rock and gravel road below. I quickly unslung my day pack, changed from my snowboarding boots into my hiking boots, and reshouldered my day pack. Strapping my snowboard onto my back, I ran down the snowy slope after him. The two of us thus began our journey to the Thunderbolt Monastery, to meet the mysterious Oracle who lived there.

As we hiked down the road into the Nepalese sunset, we talked. The soft pastel hues of red and purple began to darken in the Himalayan sky above us.

Though Master Fwap was a Tibetan Buddhist monk, he was well versed in a variety of different schools of Buddhism. In one of our very first conversations, he had explained to me why he freely drew techniques and understandings from different Buddhist traditions.

Many Buddhist masters confined themselves to a single Buddhist school of teachings, but it was his feeling that staying within a particular Buddhist school was not that important. He believed that an individual who studied Buddhist yoga and meditation should learn all of what he referred to as the "branches" of the "tree of Buddhist knowledge." He admonished me to learn and employ whichever Buddhist techniques I found worked best for me, regardless of whether they were from the Tibetan, Zen, or any other Buddhist school.

The early evening air grew even colder, so I pulled my parka around me tightly. Master Fwap resumed his ongoing conversation about Zen and the art of snowboarding.

"Before you start snowboarding down a mountain," he began, shifting to a more formal tone, "visualize that you and your snowboard are part of a singular globe of light. Then, as you descend the slope, continue to hold that image firmly in your mind."

He chuckled. "Naturally you must keep your eyes open! Watch where you are going at all times! When you first start to practice mindfulness, you will occasionally be distracted and forget to practice your visualization technique. Try not to be frustrated when this happens. When you are distracted and forget, simply revisualize the globe of light and then hold its image in your mind. Once you have become comfortable with this technique, you will be ready for the second and more advanced part of this visualization. I did not mention this more advanced part of the technique to you when we were last together, because I wanted you to have a chance to become proficient in the basic visualization first.

"While you are snowboarding down a mountain," he continued, "stretch out your feelings and awareness as far as you can. Reach out and touch the web of life around you."

"What is the web of life, and how would I visualize touching it?" I asked, breathing hard. We were ascending a high pass, and the cold, thin air made it difficult for me to hike and talk simultaneously. My curiosity was now aroused by his description of the second part of the technique. I didn't know if I could successfully visualize what he had described while plummeting down mountains of snow and ice, but if it would help me advance my snowboarding skills, I would definitely give it a try.

Master Fwap looked at me for a moment when we finally reached the top of the pass. Then he laughed as he answered my question. "In Zen Buddhist philosophy, all of life is considered to be holy. It is the Zen belief that all individual manifestations of life are interconnected by invisible lines of energy. These lines of energy intimately connect everything in the universe to everything else, in and through the astral and causal dimensions."

We walked down the other side of the pass in silence for several minutes. The sun had now completely disappeared behind the mountains. The only light that enabled us to see where we were walking was the bright, white halo that surrounded the jagged, snow-covered western peaks above us and then reflected down onto the snow-covered road we were traversing.

"Don't indulge yourself with feelings of guilt or recrimination," Master Fwap said, returning to our earlier topic of conversation. "Be calm and stay centered, and then start practicing the technique again.

"It is a good idea to avoid judging your progress whenever you practice any type of yogic meditation technique. The reason for this is simple—Buddhist yoga is beyond the mind's understanding."

"What do you mean by that?"

"When you practice a meditation technique, you are learning to interact with both the hidden portions of yourself and those of the universe. The latter exist in the nonphysical dimension."

"But," I interjected, "isn't it important to gauge your progress when you are learning any new skill? If you don't know how well you are doing something, how can you know whether you should be trying to do it better, or if you should modify or radically change your approach?"

"The study of Buddhist yoga," Master Fwap began, "or of any mystical practice or discipline that takes you above body consciousness, should be approached in a nonconceptual way. Then the result of using the technique will be the practice itself."

"How can the result be the practice itself? The reason you practice an art in the first place is to gain something from it, isn't it?"

Master Fwap laughed gently, rhythmically shaking his head from side to side. He then gave me one of his all-knowing Buddhist monk smiles before responding, "The purpose of Buddhist yoga is to become enlightened. But enlightenment is not just one thing. Of course there is total enlightenment, which is the melding of your mind with nirvana. But there are also countless other small enlightening experiences, which I refer to as 'epiphanies.'"

"What is an epiphany?" I inquired, as I sidestepped a large group of stones that had fallen into the center of the mountain road.

"An epiphany is a powerful mystical experience. An epiphany occurs when you make a brief excursion beyond your physical body and mind, and travel into a dimension of light. During that journey your mind transcends the normal categorical states of consciousness that it usually perceives time and space through, and, for a timeless time, it perceives reality in nonordinary ways. An epiphany is usually also the catalyst for a metamorphosis in your day-to-day consciousness. You are never quite the same after having experienced one. After you have an epiphany, your mind gains a new and better understanding of both yourself and the universe you live in."

"But what does having an epiphany have to do with Buddhist yoga being the result of being the practice itself?" I asked in a frustrated tone of voice. At this point, Master Fwap had totally lost me, and I hoped he would explain what he had just said.

"Consider snowboarding, for a moment. Why do you snowboard? You snowboard because your practice is your result. Or, to put it another way, you enjoy doing it simply because you are doing

. Practicing Buddhist yoga is similar. People practice Buddhist yoga because they enjoy the experiences they have during the period of time they are practicing."

We walked on in silence for some time. The moon had started to rise and provided ample light for us to maneuver.

"When you are meditating, your higher mind is reaching out and touching the web of life. During meditation you touch higher dimensions of consciousness. These dimensions cause you to experience power, ecstasy, and knowledge during the minutes you are meditating. The feelings that you have while meditating are often renewing and wonderful! So the point of practicing meditation is to experience the heightened feelings that come from this new awareness. Do you understand?"

"I think so, Master Fwap," I replied in an unsure voice. "You are saying that people meditate because it makes them feel good while they are meditating."

"That is correct," he immediately responded. "It feels wonderful to meditate. Nothing feels better! And after a person has finished meditating, the mind is relaxed, at peace, and filled with bright, luminous energy."

"Okay, I can understand that part, but what does this all have to do with not knowing how I am progressing in my practice, and then what does that have to do with epiphanies?"

"You do have a wonderful way of confusing yourself, don't you?" Master Fwap inquired with a soft smile.

I didn't reply. I knew that if I said anything more at this point I would only confuse myself further.

"This is really not so difficult to understand," Master Fwap continued. "Let me try to simplify all of this for you: We have two sides, that's all."

"What do you mean by that?"

"We have two bodies. We all have a physical body through which we perceive and interact with the physical universe, and we also have an energy body through which we perceive and interact with the nonphysical dimensions.

The problem is that our physical body and mind are blatantly unaware of our nonphysical side. You see, our physical person is really the smaller of our two bodies. Our nonphysical side is infinitely greater; it exists simultaneously in many different dimensions. Our nonphysical side is ancient, powerful, and knowledgeable. It is the part of us that exists from one incarnation to another. Within it is housed everything that you have learned in all of your past lives. When you can bring the awareness of your nonphysical body into your day-to-day consciousness, you become a happier and more powerful person."

"But what does that awareness have to do with not judging my progress in meditation?"

"Hmm? Oh, I was just getting to that. Your physical mind cannot possibly grasp the true nature of your nonphysical body. It simply doesn't have the capacity to do so. It can, however, become aware that your nonphysical body exists, and it can also learn to appreciate its help. The world is not really what it seems to be at all. By that I mean that life is not reasonable. It just is. As thinking beings, we have grown accustomed to explaining life to ourselves as a reasonable process. But that is simply our default as reasoning beings and not necessarily a true and correct perception of the way things actually are."

"What do you mean by that?"

"Okay, for example, when you put on a pair of colored sunglasses, the world that greets your eyes changes color. Your colored sunglasses superimpose a colored tint over everything you see. When you remove your sunglasses, you again see the world in its normal

Life is what it is, but our reasoning mind and sense ‚ tint what we perceive. Meditation, be it passive or ac- ‚ is simply a way of seeing and experiencing life directly, without any mental modifications, or, to put it another way, without any sunglasses on. Your physical mind cannot see into the invisible realms of consciousness; it simply doesn't have the ability to do so."

Master Fwap paused for a moment before continuing.

"Since your progression in meditation takes place in the non-physical dimensions—which are beyond your physical mind's perceptions—your physical mind simply can't know how you are doing. Any thoughts or judgments you might have about your progression in meditation are purely conjecture and should be disregarded. While your physical mind may not be able to chart your progression into the nonphysical dimensions, it can pragmatically appreciate your meditative journeys."

"How?" I asked. "I thought you just said that my physical mind can't know whether I am progressing in meditation. If that's true, how can it appreciate whether meditation is beneficial to me?"

"Because it can see the results," Master Fwap replied, with a satisfied look on his face. "Your mind can see that meditating regularly makes you happier and more at peace with yourself, and that it also improves your ability to do just about anything more successfully and happily, including snowboarding! While your physical mind might not understand exactly what is going on with your nonphysical side, it can accept and embrace your practice of meditation because it can logically see the benefits for its physical self.

"When you first start to practice meditation and mindfulness," Master Fwap went on, "you should not look for a quick result. As a matter of fact, when you first start practicing, you will probably feel that you are accomplishing nothing and simply wasting your time. But if you continue to practice in spite of these internal doubts, after a few months you will begin to have more energy, feel happier, and be better at almost everything you do! As you become more adept at meditating and your practice improves, you will start to have ecstatic experiences while you are meditating. The process itself will then become its own reward."

"So, Master Fwap, if I understand what you are saying correctly, in the beginning, practicing mindfulness while I am snowboarding is a faith thing, and I should just do it, even though it won't seem to be making that much of a difference in how I feel or snowboard?"

"That is correct. Give it six months. After that, I think that you will be rather pleasantly surprised."

"So what does meditation have to do with the epiphanies you mentioned?" We had just rounded the corner of a mountain, and in its shadow I couldn't see Master Fwap very well as he answered my question.

"Epiphanies are strong meditative experiences. Initially, you will have them when you are meditating, but after you have practiced meditation for several years, your consciousness will become more lucid and you will be able to journey to the other dimensions any time you want or need to."

"So an epiphany is a journey into the other dimensions?" I asked. "How is that different from meditation?"

"Meditation is a process by which you stop your physical thoughts. When your physical thoughts stop, the world stops, and time and space dissolve into essence.

"Let's just say that an epiphany is a very strong meditative experience—an exceptional meditative experience. During an epiphany you go beyond your normal level of meditation—in which you are consciously experiencing higher dimensional light and ecstasy—and you become the experience you are experiencing."

"But wait . . . If you become the thing that you are experiencing, then you can't be 'you' anymore, and therefore you can't know what you are experiencing, or even that you are having an experience."

"Yes, normally I would agree with you. Except that you are forgetting just one thing."

"What is that?"

"An entirely different 'you' might be conscious of its own experience."

"I don't get it. Give me an example."

"Well, suppose you were snowboarding down a mountain, and you were practicing mindfulness. Suddenly, your awareness left this world and went to the other side, into the nonphysical dimensions. There your mind merged with a higher dimension of intelligent light, and you then became that dimension.

"And let us further suppose," Master Fwap continued, as we rounded the corner of the mountain and were, much to my relief, bathed again in the Nepalese moonlight, "that the dimension you became had an independent awareness of its own, an awareness that was far beyond human awareness, an awareness that apprehended life in a totally different way than you are accustomed to. Then you would be aware of your experience as that dimension, only it would be a different 'you' that would be aware of it."

"What would happen to my body while my mind went to the other side and assumed a different awareness? Wouldn't I fall off my snowboard and get hurt or killed?"

"No. If you were having a real epiphany, you would be just fine. Your body would continue to do everything perfectly, actually even more perfectly than normal, while your conscious awareness was elsewhere."

"But when I came back to being me again, would I remember going to the other side, or would I remember snowboarding down the mountain?"

"No, you wouldn't remember either experience, at least not in the way that you are normally used to remembering things. Your experience on the other side would be only a vague recollection of bright and beautiful light to you, nothing more. And you would suddenly find yourself back in your physical body again, without remembering what your body's experience had been while your conscious awareness was on the other side."

"I kind of understand what you mean, Master Fwap. Sometimes when I am driving on the interstates of California I forget that I am driving. Particularly when I am driving from L.A. to San Francisco. Suddenly I realize that I just drove fifty miles successfully, but I don't remember having done it. Is that similar to what you are describing?"

"Yes, your body is directing your car perfectly, while another part of you is traveling through the interdimensional planes."

"What's the point, then? If I wouldn't get to enjoy experiencing the other side, or this side, during an epiphany, why bother?"

"Oh, but you would experience both sides! It just depends on which 'you' we are talking about. Your physical person would enjoy the feelings of snowboarding, just as it does normally. And your nonphysical self would enjoy itself to the utmost while it journeyed into and became one with one of the dimensions of higher intelligent light."

"But where would I be during all of this?"

"Why, you would be in both places at once."

"But you said that I wouldn't remember either experience, and that I wouldn't even know that I was having, or had, them."

"Well, I suppose it depends on who you are, doesn't it?"

"What do you mean by that?"

"Well, suppose you are your physical body, and at the same time you are a different you in other dimensions, as well."

"But what about the me that is talking to you now. Isn't this who I really am?"

"No, of course not. The you that is speaking to me now isn't the real you at all."

"But how can that be true? I am me, aren't I?"

"Not according to Buddhist yoga," Master Fwap smiled. "The whole point of practicing yoga is to discover that we are someone or something completely different from who or what we thought we were. As long as you conceive of yourself as a person in dimensional space, you are trapped in an inaccurate description of yourself and—to return to my earlier analogy—you are seeing the world and yourself through tinted glasses. As you progress in your meditation practice, you will come to discover that you are much more complicated than you had ever imagined yourself to be! The 'you' that you refer to as yourself is at best only a thin veneer; it is a mask that prevents you from knowing and being all that you really are. Through the practice of Buddhist yoga, we gradually remove the mask of personality. We find out that beneath our mask of personality we have an infinite variety of selves within us.

As your famous American poet, Walt Whitman, said, we 'contain multitudes.' Continue your practice of mindfulness and meditation. Don't worry about how you are doing, just do it! Remember, the only bad type of practice is when you don't practice at all. In time you will discover your other selves, and eventually you will discover the deepest part of your being, nirvana, which is, of course, wonderful beyond your mind's understanding.

"Keep practicing, and in time you will be able to become consciously one with your snowboard—or anything else, for that matter. Remember, the trick with any type of meditation is simply to keep trying, even if it doesn't seem like you are making any progress at all."

3

I Meet the Oracle

After several hours of hiking over some of the most beautiful moon-lit terrain I had ever seen in the Himalayas, we came to the Oracle's temple. It was perched on the side of a cliff. In the pale moonlight it looked very old and had seemingly fallen into a state of disrepair. Mortar had fallen from the sides of the building's entrance, and the red and orange paint around the wooden entrance had heavily faded.

Master Fwap told me that just below the cliff monastery there were wheat and barley fields. He said that on a clear day it was often possible to see beyond the fields to the rhododendron forest, where tigers and other exotic animals roamed freely.

Master Fwap walked up to the temple door, opened it, and walked inside. I followed in his footsteps with a great deal of trep-idation.

The entrance we passed through led into a small meditation room that was lit with dozens of red and white candles in open-topped jars. The altar at the front of the room was filled with old Buddha statues. A large, faded Buddhist painting of some gods and goddesses joined in sexual union hung above the altar. I had never seen anything quite like it in the other temples that Master Fwap and I had visited in our previous travels. After looking at it, I suddenly felt like getting laid.

Unlike the clean, neat, and well-kept temples Master Fwap and I had visited on our previous adventures together, the Oracle's temple was definitely, in my opinion, in need of a heavy makeover.

Master Fwap smiled as he watched me look over the scene. Then he began to speak in a soft but purposeful tone of voice. "I think you have an expression in your language about not judging a book by its cover, don't you?" he inquired rhetorically. "Well, the Oracle and his temple are different from anything you have seen in Nepal yet, so postpone your judgment of the surface reality you see around you and listen carefully to anything he says when he arrives, if he chooses to speak with you."

Master Fwap gestured that we should both sit on some meditation cushions in front of the altar. We had been sitting for only a few minutes when the Oracle noiselessly arrived.

He was tall and thin and was wearing an ocher monk's robe with a red sash wrapped around its middle. He was younger than Master Fwap; I judged him to be in his late forties. He wore several sets of heavy white and black stone beads around his neck.

His eyes darted back and forth between Master Fwap and me, and his facial expression seemed to change every few seconds. He would alternately be calm, then laugh, and then shout something in a language I couldn't understand, and then be calm again. Then he wept. He got down on his knees and bowed his head, touching the floor with his forehead, in the direction of the altar at the front of the room.

He looked crazy to me.

I glanced over at Master Fwap, looking for a cue from him as to how I should act or what I should ask, but he had closed his eyes and was engaged in meditation. I was at a complete loss as to what to do. One thing I knew for sure was that I was definitely out of my league.

The Oracle lifted his head from his bow, stood up, and excitedly ran over to me. I was so surprised that I fell backward off my cushion! Both the Oracle and Master Fwap started laughing hysterically as I got up off the stone floor and sat back down on my meditation cushion.

"At last you have come, at last, at last," the crazy monk mumbled to me in broken English. He stared directly into my eyes. It was intense. His eyes were filled with light; they were like two diamonds on fire. I was mesmerized by them. Then he laughed a crazy loonlike laugh and ran around the room three times.

He then stopped in front of Master Fwap, bowed to him, and said in perfect English, "Welcome, Enlightened One, to my humble home. I see I have scared your young disciple. You have not told him about my ways, evidently. Another one of your practical jokes, perhaps?"

Then both he and Master Fwap started to laugh together until tears were streaming down their faces. All I could do was watch in amazement.

The Oracle suddenly became silent. He closed his eyes and seemed to be meditating. As I watched him standing in front of Master Fwap, the room felt as if it were becoming charged with static electricity. Then what I perceived at first as a vague blue electric light began to emanate from and surround the Oracle's body.

I rubbed my eyes in disbelief, but it was still there! The Oracle's entire body was surrounded by a clear and well-defined electric azure blue aura.

The Oracle opened his eyes slowly. He suddenly turned and faced me. His eyes had lost their diamondlike brightness and instead they now appeared to have grown cold and birdlike. He began to chant something in another language that I couldn't understand.

After chanting for several minutes, he began rhythmically to rock his body back and forth as if he were in some type of trance.

Then he spoke. Rapidly, and with a singsong tone, he said that he now embodied an ancient master, a master who wished to speak to me, a master who used to live in India and Tibet and who had been my master in past lives. He said that he had a message for me.

At this point, I didn't know if the Oracle and Master Fwap were having a joke at my expense or not, but the Oracle's sparkling aura, coupled with the electric charge I felt in the air, convinced me that something highly unusual was indeed happening and that I had better pay attention. I sat up straight and listened carefully to what the Oracle said to me.

"You have come to the Himalayas to see and feel all of the beauty and ecstasy that are within you. It is easier here, where there are fewer human auras and the interdimensional planes can still be accessed.

"You might ask yourself why you snowboard. When you snowboard you purify yourself. You are concentrating while you are on the holy mountains of power and you are unconsciously merging with the higher dimensions as you snowboard through them.

"But you must now go to the Anapurna range—the dimensions are closing there now. You must go in several days. I will accompany you, as will Master Fwap. With our combined power we can still open the dimensions there for you and show you their secrets . . . but we must go soon or it will be too late."

His head dropped and his eyes snapped shut. The blue aura that had been surrounding his body gradually faded and then disappeared.

The Oracle opened his eyes, raised his head, and then ceremoniously stood up. He left the room, walking swiftly and lightly and with great dignity, leaving Master Fwap and me alone.

"What was that all about, Master Fwap?" I inquired hastily.

"Oh, that," Master Fwap said thoughtfully. "The Oracle gave you your first insight. You must do as he says, we both must. We shall accompany you to the Anapurna Himalayas. There the two of us will open the dimensions, and you will discover their secrets."

"But wait a minute here. With all due respect to you and your friend, I came here to snowboard, not to learn about any missing dimensions."

"You will have plenty of opportunity to snowboard where we are going. But tomorrow, after you have slept in the safety of the Oracle's temple, you must return to Katmandu. Stay there for several days and rest and enjoy yourself. Oh, by the way, while you are in Katmandu, you will meet someone, a woman you knew in several of your past lives.

"After you have rested and have had your encounter with her, come to my temple on the outskirts of Katmandu. The Oracle and I will be waiting for you. Oh, and the Oracle gave me something for you to read between now and then. I think you might find it helpful."

Master Fwap reached inside his robe and pulled out a small cloth-bound book. As he handed it to me, he laughed and said, "Don't worry, it's not written in Sanskrit as it once was. It has been translated into English by one of the younger monks."

I looked down at the book, and in the temple's soft candlelight I could barely make out its title. In black, handwritten letters it said, *The Handbook for Enlightenment.*

I didn't see the Oracle again for the rest of the evening. Master Fwap escorted me to a room at the rear of the temple where he said I could spend the night.

The room was small, clean, and comfortable. It had a tiny cot, an altar with a Buddha statue on it, and a small dresser for clothes.

On all four of the walls were Tibetan *thanka* paintings, which depicted various beings engaged in sexual congress. I decided that it would be best to wait until another time to ask about their religious meaning.

I was curious about the idea of meeting a woman in Katmandu in the next few days whom Master Fwap said I had known in many of my past lives, and I also wanted some time to myself.

The Oracle was simply too weird, and I was beginning to suspect that he and Master Fwap had cooked up some type of scheme to get me to join their Buddhist order. I was definitely not interested in anything like that. I had come to the Himalayas for the ultimate snowboarding challenge, not to be converted to Buddhism.

I undressed quickly after Master Fwap left my room. I washed my hands and face with some water that was provided in a bowl on the dresser. Then I quickly slid into bed and covered myself with all of the old woolen blankets that were at the foot of the cot. The room was freezing.

Before blowing out the candles in the room, I took a look at the book the Oracle had given to me. On the surface it didn't look particularly impressive. I opened it and saw that it was all handwritten and in English. It appeared to be more of a diary than a book. I was just about to start reading it when Master Fwap slipped into the room.

He stood over me without saying anything for a moment, then he asked me if there was anything that the Oracle had said that I hadn't understood.

I thought for a minute and replied, "Yes, there are a couple of things. Both the Oracle and the voice I heard up on the mountain today talked about the dimensions changing, about their being missing, or closing, or something. Can you explain any of this to me?"

"Yes, surely. It is not complicated at all," he replied in a soft, soothing voice. "You see, the universe is filled with an endless number of dimensions. Most people are aware of only the first three. In Buddhist yoga we learn about, travel into, and experience many, many other dimensions.

"The problem is the earth's population. As you and I have discussed before, every human being has an aura. A person's aura acts like a radio transmitter. It sends impressions into the psychic planes of our planet. If there are too many auras in one place, they tend to pollute the psychic environment of an area, like the smog often does to the air in your Los Angeles."

"I know exactly what you mean. On a clear day in L.A., I can see the San Bernadino mountains from the 405 freeway, or if I am surfing at Zuma Beach in Malibu, I can see Catalina and the Santa Barbara Channel Islands. But most of the time it is smoggy in L.A. and I can't see them. If it weren't for the occasional clear days, when the Santa Ana winds blow, I would never even know that they existed."

"Exactly!" Master Fwap said in an exalted tone of voice. "So it is the same with the dimensions. The population of the earth is now almost six billion and increasing faster every day. Some dimensions that we used to see have literally become invisible. You can walk up to them and not even know they are there, let alone be able to enter into them, learn their secrets, and have enlightening and empowering experiences traveling through them.

"The Oracle and I have power. We have been Tantric Buddhist monks for many years, and we were taught by our masters how to travel into and through the interdimensional planes. It is your karma

32

to learn this art, to enter into those dimensions and learn their secrets. But we must do it quickly, because even with our help, it will be difficult. There are things you must learn here in the Himalayas. Your past karma in Buddhist practice has caused you to return here to regain your enlightenment from your past lives. You are what we Tibetans refer to as a *tulku*."

"A *tulku?*" I asked. My fatigue had suddenly vanished. I sat up on the cot, wrapping the woolen blankets around me to hear his explanation.

"A *tulku*," he replied, "is an advanced soul that has practiced yoga and meditation in many of its former lives. Some *tulkus* are enlightened, some are close to enlightenment. In your case, as I have told you before, you have been enlightened in many of your past lives. But you must regain your past-life knowledge and enlightenment.

"It is the Oracle's and my job to help you accomplish this. It is the dharma, which is a Buddhist way of saying this is simply the way it is. Both of us have seen this in our meditation.

"Your snowboarding is a type of meditation for you. When you snowboard down mountains with powerful auras, you are in a state of total concentration. This causes you to access the aura and power of the mountain, in much the same way that a Buddhist monk does when he sits in meditation on such a mountain and concentrates on the dimensions.

"The Hindu Kush, particularly around Anapurna, is rapidly becoming aurically polluted. Many trekkers and mountain climbers who do not respect these sacred sites are, as you would say, 'trashing' them.

"It is imperative that we take you with us there, immediately. With our combined power we can open the dimensions around Anapurna and allow you to explore their secrets. If we wait much longer, it will not be possible. The area is becoming more and more polluted every month. It will be challenging for the both of us to do this for you even now.

"Get some sleep. You have quite an interesting encounter waiting for you back in Katmandu," he said with an all-knowing grin. "Study the book the Oracle has given you between now and then. It will help you understand a great deal of this. Now sleep. You have a long journey ahead of you tomorrow."

Master Fwap left the room unceremoniously, gently closing the door behind him.

After he left, I picked up the handwritten book he had handed me earlier. It looked innocuous enough. I opened *The Handbook for Enlightenment* and flipped to a page in the middle of the book.

> You are not what you think. What you think changes, like all of life. You are what you don't think.
>
> Life is a journey of the spirit. Don't fight it, go with it. There is nothing you can do about it, anyway, so why not be happy?
>
> Beyond this world there are countless worlds, and beyond them lies nirvana. It is perfect awareness beyond self.
>
> Don't be afraid of the truths of life. Hard though they might be to understand, and troubling though your experiences may be in this or any incarnation, the truths set forth in this book will free you. They are the composite knowledge of all the great Tantric Buddhist

masters who have successfully walked the path between the worlds that you are now traversing. You too
will succeed.

   Meditate on these thoughts and you will come to
know all that can be said in words. The rest you must
experience in meditation. May your journey on the path
of the razor's edge be filled with light and success. May
all sentient beings attain enlightenment! May the
dharma conquer all ignorance!

At this point, fatigue began to consume me like an avalanche in
the Himalayas. I just couldn't read anymore. I placed the book
down by my side, put my head on the pillow, and fell into a
dreamless sleep. I slept peacefully in the Oracle's monastery until
sunrise.

4

The Handbook for Enlightenment

The next day I awakened to a freezing dawn. I got out of bed and hastily put on my clothes and down parka. I was very hungry.

The candles I had left lit when I had fallen asleep had burned themselves out, and the only light in the room was the faint, cold gray light of dawn that filtered in through some makeshift windows covered with old plastic.

After leaving my room I proceeded to make my way down the hall. Entering the meditation room, I saw Master Fwap and the Oracle sitting in front of the altar engaged in meditation.

Moving as silently as I could, I walked up behind them, sat down, assumed a cross-legged position, and tried to meditate with them.

It was easy at first. My mind was completely at rest and I didn't think at all. Then I began to feel hungry. No matter how hard I tried to make my mind quiet and continue to meditate, I kept picturing every type of breakfast food imaginable. I thought of scrambled eggs and buttered toast, pancakes dripping with syrup, hash browns, orange juice, milk, coffee, cereal, and even Pop-Tarts. Then my stomach began to growl.

It was awful. The high ceilings of the stone meditation room amplified the gurgling sounds of my stomach. Here I was in the presence of two aged Buddhist monks who were engaged in deep meditation, visualizing American breakfast foods.

Master Fwap and the Oracle then began giggling, and what started out as chuckles quickly progressed to howls of laughter. They both turned and looked at me with tears in their eyes. I was really embarrassed, to say the least.

Simultaneously they became silent and stared at me. As they stared I began to feel a pleasantly warm tingling sensation that filled my body and numbed my senses. My mind became quiet. All thoughts of food and hunger vanished, and I found myself closing my eyes, stopping my thoughts, and effortlessly meditating again.

When I reopened my eyes, Master Fwap and the Oracle were touching their heads to the cold stone floor, signaling that their morning meditation period had ended. I did my best to emulate their bows, touching the stone floor with my forehead. While I still didn't understand the purpose of all of the bowing that everyone did in Nepal, I figured it was polite to go along with it.

Then Master Fwap and the Oracle stood up, stretched, and told me that it was time to go to the kitchen for something to eat.

We all walked down a dark and narrow corridor to the back of the Oracle's temple, where we entered a small room that contained an old wooden table, several chairs, and a fireplace. The Oracle proceeded to light a small fire in the fireplace and then hung an old metal kettle on a hook over the flames. Master Fwap disappeared into a small pantry and quickly returned with bread, butter, and cheese. When the tea was ready, the three of us sat down at the table together.

The Oracle poured the tea while Master Fwap gave us each large portions of bread, cheese, and butter on some worn-out china plates. All of this was done in complete silence. The only sounds to be heard were the first songbirds of morning and Master Fwap's quiet humming.

After eating in silence for several minutes, Master Fwap began: "Today you will go to Katmandu. It is a long journey. When you become tired, sit and rest, and read a little from the book I gave you last night. It will refresh you and renew your strength.

"The young woman you will meet tonight in Katmandu is someone you have known in many of your past lives. You two have been very close before, as I am sure you will be again." A sudden grin appeared on his face as he said this, and then both he and the crazy Oracle began to weep again with laughter.

"Once you have become close," he said while trying to suppress his grin, "come to my monestery. The Oracle and I will be waiting for you there. Then the three of us will begin our journey to the Anapurna range, where we will help you to solve the riddle of the missing dimensions."

I thanked both the Oracle and Master Fwap for their hospitality. The Oracle then laughed, jumped up from his chair, and without warning leaped effortlessly onto the top of the table. He swiftly raised both of his arms toward the ceiling and started taking in a series of very intense deep breaths. I was dumbfounded by both his antics and the effortlessness of his jump.

As an extreme snowboarder, I knew a lot about jumping, and I didn't understand how the Oracle could move the way he just had. But before I could give the matter more thought, he lowered both of his arms, aimed his outstretched palms at me, and made a loud blowing sound.

It was as if I were hit by a lightning bolt! Everything in my visual field went white, and I was knocked off my chair and onto the cold stone floor beneath me. I tried getting back up, but my muscles wouldn't work. All I could do was to lie on my back and listen to Master Fwap's and the Oracle's crazy peels of laughter. After several minutes the white light faded and the room came back to normal. I was able to sit up again. Master Fwap and the Oracle were still chuckling at my expense, and I immediately decided that this had all gotten too weird for me. Somehow I managed to get up on to my feet and leave the room as rapidly as possible.

I ran back to my room, got my snowboard and backpack, and was about to leave when I remembered the book. Turning back to the bed, I grabbed *The Handbook for Enlightenment*, stuffed it into my backpack, and left the room.

After leaving the temple, I started down the hill toward the rock and gravel road. As I walked down the grassy hill toward the road that led to Katmandu, I ventured a quick backward glance over my shoulder at the Oracle's temple. Master Fwap and the crazy Oracle were standing at the temple's front door, still laughing and waving farewell to me. I waved back and rapidly walked down to the road.

I spent the next several hours jogging. Whatever the Oracle had done to me in the kitchen had filled me with energy. I was literally running up and down seventeen- and eighteen-thousand-foot passes as if I were Superman.

After about three hours, I suddenly became very tired. I had reached the top of a particularly gnarly snow- and ice-covered pass, when I suddenly felt that if I didn't sit down and rest immediately, I would pass out.

Unshouldering my backpack and snowboard, I lay down. I was dizzy with waves of exhaustion. It was then that I noticed that my clothes were completely soaked through with perspiration.

I wasn't so sure that the Superman empowerment, or whatever it was that the Oracle had done that had charged me up with so much energy in the kitchen, was such a good idea.

Then I remembered Master Fwap's advice about the book the Oracle had given me. I fished around inside my backpack until I found it. Looking at it in the clear light of day, it seemed less impressive than it had by candlelight in the Oracle's monastery the evening before. I opened the book to the first page and began to read.

Oh, nobly born. In your hands you hold the distillation of the wisdom of the great Tantric Masters of the Rae Chorze-Fwaz Order of Tibetan Tantric Yoga.

Because of your good karma from past ages, you have found your way back to the path. This book is the distilled elixir of dharma practices. Pay close attention to that which follows. It will lead you on the short path to the clear light of reality—the celestial state of Buddhahood, where the world as you know it will stop, and the pain of sentient existence will come to an end.

Be diligent in your practice. Be patient. You will succeed in your task in this world. Your task is consciously to rejoin the stream of perfect consciousness that abides both in and around all things.

Once you have accomplished this, you may choose to pass into oblivion—nirvana—for all time. Or you may choose to stay in the dimensional worlds to play or to help others along the pathway to enlightenment. The choice will be yours. May your path be filled with great joy!

After reading the introduction, I closed the book and placed it on my snowboard. I lay my head back against my backpack, closed my eyes, and relaxed.

I must have fallen asleep for a few minutes. I found myself in a dream. In my dream I was back in the youth hostel in Katmandu. I was sitting upright on my sleeping bag, and across from me was the most beautiful woman I had ever seen.

She had long blond hair that ran halfway down her back. Her skin was pale and smooth. She wore a turtleneck sweater and blue jeans. Her tight, white spandex turtleneck sweater sinuously revealed her firm, prominent breasts. She was thin-waisted and definitely very sexy.

She smiled playfully at me and then took my hand and held it. As she did, I felt an electric pulse flow between our two bodies.

"You are coming to me," she said. "It will not be long now. I have waited for you for many lives. It is our time again."

She took my hand, raised it, and allowed me to touch her breasts. Then she raised my hand and placed it on her heart. Suddenly I was engulfed with warm and happy emotions.

A series of scenes then began to pass before my mind's eye. In the scenes I saw the two of us together, but we were in different bodies and in a different dimension. We were sitting by a large river. She was dressed in a purplish robe. We sat together without talking, watching the boats with their multicolored blue and white sails quietly moving along the river.

Sitting next to her, I felt as if we were one being in two bodies. There was a timeless feeling, as if the two of us had always been sitting here, by this river, together, in this dimension, and always would be, no matter where our physical bodies might be.

I turned and looked at her. Her eyes shined with the brightness of the sun on a cloudless day. I was overpowered by love, but this seemed strange to me. I don't think I had really ever loved anyone, except for Master Fwap and a few of my snowboarding buddies. I had certainly never felt this close to a woman before.

Before I had a chance to consider this matter further, I woke up. Strange dream, I thought.

I stood up, stretched and yawned, and then after reshouldering my gear, I started hiking at a much slower pace toward Katmandu.

After several hours of hiking, I took another break. It was around one o'clock in the afternoon. I figured I had covered about half the distance to Katmandu. Sitting down on some meadow grass, I decided to check out *The Handbook for Enlightenment* again.

I pulled it out of my backpack and opened it to the first chapter, "The Short Way of Meditation."

> Meditation is a practice of making your mind still. Stillness is your mind's natural state. It is only when you become agitated by your surroundings, by things that you desire or fear, that you lose your natural state of mental equilibrium and fall into confusing and degenerate lower states of mind.
>
> Your mind should always be engaged in meditation; strive to make it happy, calm, centered, and still. Unhappiness, fear, depression, and frustration are unnatural states of mind. They are the result of leaving your mind's innate state of enlightenment.
>
> The world around you changes constantly. There is little or nothing you can do about it. Try! Change the world today to what you want or how you think it

42

should be. If you are able to do this, you will discover in a short while that everything you have changed will change again into something different and that you will be frustrated and disappointed by this.

This is not to suggest that you should be passive in your life. It is important to have goals and to strive for the things in life that you are naturally drawn to. The important point to understand is not to get attached to what you want to have happen to yourself or others, or to the events and outcomes that you wish to occur in this or any other incarnation.

Try your best to be your best. Meditate and quiet your mind. Then you will always know what the dharma is—that which is spiritually correct for yourself. By following the dharma, as opposed to your human desires and fears, you will become happy and free.

Sometimes the dharma and your desires will be in agreement. Sometimes they will not be. But you must fight always to do the right thing, whether it brings you personal gain or loss. This is the true way of Vadrayana Buddhism, the path of the awakened warrior.

The path of the awakened warrior is not an escape from reality. It is an entrance into reality. If you seek to escape from day-to-day reality, you will only increase your pain. The reality of enlightenment takes you above mental and emotional pain while you actively live in the world; reality cannot be separated from your physical life.

Samsara is nirvana: enlightenment and all of life are one. Suffering is not caused by living in the material world and having experiences here. True suffering is caused by losing touch with your inner light.

When you lose touch with your inner light you will descend into lower samsaric states of consciousness. Here you will become attached to people, places, and experiences in this and other worlds. This attachment will cause you to suffer intensely.

It is your attachment to people, places, things, desires, and fears that causes you to suffer. The daily practice of meditation will allow you to live in the world, experience the ups and downs of life, but remain unaffected by the pains and torments that attachment and aversion bring to unenlightened beings.

The correct practice of meditation will keep you in an ocean of enlightened mind that will allow you to pass freely through all of your experiences in a state of bliss. Even the normal pains that come from your physical body and mental emotions will be greatly reduced by the constant experience of inner enlightenment you will derive from the correct practice of daily meditation.

Learn to meditate well, practice, follow the advice of the true Tantric Masters, and you too will pass beyond suffering and enter into eternal happiness, bliss, ecstasy, and higher states of enlightenment—states for which there are no words.

5

Even Enlightened Girls Get
the Blues

I reached Katmandu shortly after dark. The cold windswept streets were all but empty as I made my way to the youth hostel. The Nepalese receptionist greeted me with a smile. I paid her in advance for a week's stay and then headed upstairs to the dormitory to locate the bed she had assigned to me.

The dormitory was empty. I assumed that everyone else was down on the first floor in the kitchen, preparing dinner. I realized that I had not eaten all day, and suddenly I was famished. I made my way down the stairs to the hostel's kitchen.

The smells of coriander, cumin, and other exotic spices that greeted me as I entered the kitchen told me that it was "Hurry Curry" night. One or two nights a week the hostel had a potluck dinner. Everyone staying in the hostel would contribute different vegetables, spices, breads, and grains. All the ingredients would be thrown together and cooked with Indian spices, in more of a Western fashion, skipping the painstaking rituals usually associated with the proper preparation of traditional Indian curries.

I joined my fellow travelers just as they were beginning to serve dinner. I contributed money, since I had not brought any of the food that night.

I sat down at a table with a couple of guys who had come

from England, and they told me that they had come to Nepal to do some serious mountain climbing. The weather in the higher Himalayas had been bad for the past few days and had forced them to stay indoors.

Without trying to look too obvious, I scanned the room for the young woman Master Fwap had mentioned I was going to encounter at the hostel. But aside from a woman from Sweden who was sitting contentedly with her boyfriend, I didn't see anyone who fit Master Fwap's description.

After finishing dinner and helping to clean up and wash the dishes, I went back upstairs to the dormitory. I thought I would read a little more from *The Handbook for Enlightenment* and then crash. I had decided that Master Fwap was obviously wrong about my meeting a woman from my past lives, and I was already mentally preparing myself to go snowboarding the next day.

I lay down on my cot, reached over, and picked up *The Handbook.* I was just about to start the second chapter, "The Preliminary Meditation Practices," when I heard someone lie down on the bunk next to me.

I glanced over to see who it was, secretly hoping it wasn't going to be a snoring British mountain climber, but much to my shock and amazement it was her! It was the blond woman I had seen in my dream earlier in the afternoon. She was even in the blue jeans and white turtleneck sweater I had seen her in.

"This is too weird," I muttered to myself as I closed the book and set it down beside the bed.

She glanced over at me with a kind of bored, sophisticated curiosity that was far different from the straightforward sexuality of American and Canadian women I had dated.

I was trying to come up with a good line, when she spoke to me, in very proper English that was highlighted with a light Danish accent. "My name is Nadia. I have come to Nepal to become enlightened. I have been here a week now, and I have visited many temples and holy places, but I have not yet met a true master. Before I came here I traveled throughout India. Again the same. I saw many buildings and many Hindu priests and yogis, but none of them seemed enlightened to me. Is this not strange? I thought when I left Denmark that this would be easy. I read many books about enlightened Hindu and Buddhist monks. But I can't find any of them.

"Before India, I was in Thailand and Japan. I asked the Zen masters I met in Japan about enlightenment and asked where I could find an enlightened master. They told me that there is an old Zen saying: 'When the student is ready, the master will appear.' So does that mean I am not ready? Is there something wrong with me?

"I don't know what to do now," she said as a pained expression crossed her face. "The only places I have not yet gone to are Tibet and Bhutan. But all the holy people have left Tibet; I met many of them in Dharmsala, India. They told me that Bhutan is the last pure place where the dharma is practiced anymore. The official state religion there is Tantric Buddhism. I don't know what to do! What are you doing in Katmandu? You are American, yes?"

As Nadia was relating her saga to me I had become entranced with her wavy blond hair, sparkling blue eyes, thick pouty lips, and curvaceous body. She was gorgeous in her clothes, and I could only imagine how much more beautiful she would be without them.

I considered telling her about my dream and about what Master Fwap and the Oracle had said about our preordained meeting. But I figured she would think that I was making it all up as a come-on and simply blow me off as a flake.

47

I opted instead for a somewhat less truthful but what I considered safer approach. "I came to Nepal to snowboard the Himalayas."

"Why would you want to do that? Are you crazy or something? If you want to snowboard, why not go to Switzerland and use the lifts? There are avalanches here all of the time."

"It's kind of hard to explain," I replied, trying not to look too obviously at her breasts.

"Well, then, tell me!"

"You see, I used to be a surfer. Then this guy invented a way to surf down a mountain on snow, using a thing call a Snurfer. I tried it and liked it. A few other people came out with the first snowboards. I tried them, and they were even better than the Snurfer.

"As the next generation or two of snowboards improved, and better boots and bindings became available, I tried snowboarding down more challenging mountains. I snowboarded just about every mountain in New England, out West, and in British Columbia. One day I woke up and just knew I had to be the first person to snowboard the Himalayas. I don't know why, but the feeling was so intense that I bought a plane ticket and just came here. I've been snowboarding the mountains here for several months now, and it is like nothing I have ever experienced."

"How do you get to the top? There are no lifts."

"I hitchhike a ride as high as I can get, then I climb from there. Then I snowsurf down a mountain and do it again."

"It sounds stupid, dangerous, and egotistical to me. If you were a mountain climber, I would understand. These are the best mountains for climbing in the world, and there are sherpa guides and experts to assist you. You Americans! You think you can just go anywhere and do anything, without proper preparation. You have no common sense!"

"Well," I quickly responded, "how sensible is it for a beautiful woman like yourself to be traveling around alone in third world countries seeking enlightenment? If you haven't noticed, life and death are pretty cheap around here."

"I am doing what my soul wants, I am following my spiritual dharma. Nothing bad can happen to me. I am being divinely protected by the powers that watch over seekers of enlightenment. I know I have been enlightened in my past lives; a monk I met told me so. If I could only find a true master, he would show me how to regain my past-life enlightenment. Nothing harmful has happened to me in all of the many dangerous places I have traveled through while trying to regain my past enlightenment."

"I think you've just been lucky, that's all. If you are so divinely protected, why haven't you met your enlightened guru or monk yet?"

She quietly sighed. I realized that I had hurt her feelings, and I felt like shit. Now, from my point of view, my encounter with her had suddenly developed a level of emotional complexity that made me feel uncomfortable. It was no longer simply a question of whether or not I was going to get laid.

I could see small tears beginning to form in her eyes. Then she looked away from me.

I tried to think of something funny to say that would cheer her up. I have never really known what to do when women cry. I'm just not very good at handling other people's emotions.

When a woman gets upset, I normally just split and call her later, after she has had some time to get herself back together. It's not that I don't want to help, but experience has taught me that whenever I try to comfort a woman in distress, I inevitably say the wrong thing and only make matters worse. For some reason, though, on that particular night it didn't seem right to walk away from Nadia and leave her alone with her tears.

What followed was a long, uncomfortable silence. I then got an idea.

"Listen, you are probably going to think that I am crazy, and I won't blame you if you do. But some very weird stuff has been happening to me since I have been here in Nepal, and it concerns a Tibetan master I met and a friend of his, this crazy Oracle guy."

"What has happened to you?" she asked with a mixed expression of curiosity and sadness.

In my best and brightest shine-on California voice, hoping to perk her up, I replied, "Well, as I mentioned before, I came to Nepal to snowboard the Himalayas. Unlike yourself, I didn't come here to become spiritually enlightened. Now I know that this is going to sound crazy, but shortly after I arrived here I had a dream in which I met a short, bald-headed Buddhist monk."

"What is so unusual about that? People have strange dreams all of the time."

"Wait, let me finish and you'll understand. Several days later, I was out snowboarding, and I ran into the monk I had seen in my dream. As a matter of fact, I snowboarded right into him. Neither of us was hurt or anything, and he said that it was all right because it was my karma to meet him that way.

"He told me that he had been my master in past lives, and his name was Master Fwap Sam-Dup. He was a Tantric Buddhist master and had formerly lived in Tibet. Master Fwap had left Tibet on the advice of his master when the Communist Chinese had invaded their country.

50

He was sent to Nepal to look for me. There was some kind of a prophecy—his master had told him that he was destined in the future to meet a young man who would come from the West. His master even told him the name of the particular mountain that he was going to encounter me on in Nepal. It was going to be his job, after his initial encounter with this young man, to teach him the secret meditation techniques of their Buddhist order. Eventually the young man would return to the West and practice the techniques for many years until he himself became enlightened. He would then transmit the secret meditation techniques of the Rae Chorze-Fwaz Order to other people in the West, by writing a series of books about the experiences he had during his youth in the Himalayas.

"I thought he was whacked and was just trying to lure me into his Buddhist order or something, but after I got to know him better, I came to realize that he *was* enlightened."

"How could you tell if he was enlightened?" Nadia asked with a new tone of curosity. I felt like I was making progress with her again.

"Well," I continued, "I don't know as much about Buddhism or enlightenment as you clearly do, but I saw Master Fwap do things that I just couldn't explain in ordinary human terms. I spent several months traveling through the Himalayas with him, and I came to respect him very much."

"What sort of things did you experience with him that were so unusual?"

"Well, to start with, I saw him turn gold. When he meditates he becomes surrounded by all of this golden light. I also saw him levitate. But most important, when I began meditating with him, I experienced his mind. He told me that it was some kind of telepathic transfer."

"What was his mind like? How did you know that it was his mind?"

"I just knew, that's all. I can't tell you how I knew, any more than I can tell you how I know that the two of us are having this conversation right now. All I can tell you is that his mind was amazing! It was made up of pure and perfect light and knowledge—it's hard to describe. When I was inside of his mind, I seemed to become part of everything in the universe. It was like I went away, and there was only eternity."

"How did you know it was eternity that you were experiencing, if, as you say, you went away?"

"I told you that this was going to be hard to explain. You are just going to have to trust me on this.

"After I had several transcendental experiences with Master Fwap, he took me to visit several Buddhist monasteries, where I met other Buddhist monks. And then just the other day he introduced me to this crazy Oracle of Nepal."

"Why, I wonder, would someone like you meet an enlightened master, and not someone like myself? I do not mean to offend you in any way, but it doesn't make sense to me. I came here to find an enlightened master, and so far I haven't been able to do so. You came to Nepal to snowboard, and you claim to have met the kind of master I have been traveling all over the world to find. It is hard for me to believe all of this. You understand this?"

"Sure, no problemo. But I can't dismiss my own experiences either. That's one of the first things that Master Fwap taught me. He said that life doesn't usually make much sense, at least not from the human point of view."

"What does that mean?" she said as she slightly shifted her head to the right, causing a rain of her blond hair to flow over her shoulders.

"The supposed incongruities of life are not really incongruities at all, according to Master Fwap. In order to understand things that don't make sense from the human point of view, it is necessary to shift our attention to a higher level of consciousness. There are thousands of different perceptual nodal points of understanding in the universe. They vary from dimension to dimension.

"He said that through the twin practices of meditation and mindfulness, a person can reach these higher points, in which confusion becomes clarity. All a person has to do is have enough personal power to get to and keep their mind in these higher-dimensional planes as they go through day-to-day life. If they can do that, then everything will make sense to them."

"Can you do that?" Nadia asked with skepticism.

"Not on a regular basis. I have discovered that I can have more powerful experiences within my own mind, through meditation. It's rad beyond belief. I mean, I'm into intensity. Before encountering Master Fwap, I thought that the most intense things in life were snowboarding, martial arts, surfing, and sex.

"I can now combine meditation with snowboarding and other physical activities. This is what is called mindfulness. I can hardly imagine what it would be like to snowboard, do martial arts, or have sex while my mind was immersed in the ecstasy and extended perceptions of higher-dimensional reality."

"You do martial arts, too?"

"Yes, I have a first-degree black belt. But I hope one day to get up to fifth or sixth."

"Why do you do this? What is so attractive about violence? Isn't there enough of it in the world already? Why make it such an important focus in your life?"

"I don't know. I guess it's because it feels so good to win. That's what my Western training teaches me, anyway. I originally got into martial arts out of necessity. I went to a pretty rough high school. There were a lot of gangs, and if you weren't a gang member—which I wasn't—some days you would get stomped pretty badly by a group of gang members. I had learned to wrestle in high school gym class, and was pretty good at it, but wrestling techniques didn't help me to defend myself against four guys grabbing and punching me out all at once. Then I saw this Bruce Lee movie, *Enter the Dragon.* I had never seen anybody move that way. Bruce Lee inspired me to try out martial arts. He seemed to be capable of megaviolence, and at the same time he was both outwardly composed and coming from a very centered place inside of his mind.

"I visited a martial arts studio in the town where I lived. There was a pretty rough crowd there, but the instructors were really cool. They could do the most fantastic things with their bodies, like double-spin kicks and breaking bricks and boards with their hands. But unlike other fighters I had met, they had a level of personal dignity and respect that I could relate to.

"I have always been interested in high-performance athletics. It's how I let off steam. I grew up in a home that had a lot of tension in it. I don't suppose that's particularly unusual in America. Most of my friends dealt with their tensions through drugs. But I just couldn't relate to that whole scene. I realized I had two choices: I could do drugs and run away from life, or I could find a better way to deal with things. A lot of my friends got into the heavy drug thing, but they looked a lot worse and were a lot unhappier after they got into drugs than they had been before.

"I also lucked out because in high school I had this great girlfriend, Jerry. She really helped me get my head together. She was an honor student, beautiful, a great dancer, and she was heavily into this Christian Science thing. She used to talk to me about it sometimes, and it sort of made sense to me."

"What religion did you grow up in?" Nadia asked.

"Well, it was kind of mixed. My father was a Roman Catholic—actually, he even studied to be a priest, but he dropped out before taking his final vows. My mother was an agnostic. She was an intellectual type, really smart. She went to Barnard College. She taught me how to read before I started going to school. I didn't see too much of her growing up, because my parents divorced when I was a kid, and she moved to another town and remarried. I ended up living with my dad.

"My two outlets growing up were athletics and reading. They got me through. I just couldn't relate to the whole Catholic thing, though. I was sent to a Catholic school for a while, and I was even an altar boy, but a lot of the Catholic things just didn't make any sense. I could relate to Jesus. But most of the Roman Catholic dogma didn't provide the answers I needed to get through my life, particularly the whole Catholic attitude toward sex."

"How's that?"

"Well, sex seems normal to me. We wouldn't be here without it, right? But the Catholic Church says that sex is the root of most human problems. According to the Catholic Church, if you have sex with someone you're not married to, you're supposed to have committed a mortal sin. If you do get married, they want you to have sex to produce lots of new Catholics for the Church.

"To be honest with you, I just don't get the marriage thing, either. Just because some guy dressed in black robes says a bunch of words while you and your bride stand before him, that's supposed to take the sin out of sex? And who is this guy anyway, and what gives him that kind of power? I have met lots of priests, and some of them have been the best people I have ever met. But some have not measured up. The whole thing with the pope is just too much for me.

"They told us in Catholic school that whatever the pope said was the word of God. They called it papal infallibility. If you study history at all, which I did when I went to public high school, you learn that a lot of the popes were corrupt. They had mistresses and did all kinds of weird stuff.

"It simply didn't make sense to me. I just couldn't buy into the whole heaven and hell thing. I mean, the whole concept that if you make a few mistakes during your life you're going to fry in hell forever is a child's fantasy. I mean, would a God of love come up with a game plan like that?"

"Do you believe in God?"

"Well, no, not really. Master Fwap says there is no God, at least not like Westerners think that there is. There is no big guy sitting in heaven judging us. Buddhists don't believe in God. Or if they do, God is nirvana; God is the universe's mind. We are all a part of it, and it is a part of us. Fwap explains all of this much better than I do.

I paused for a moment or two before continuing. "As I was saying, I had this great girlfriend in high school, Jerry. We used to ski together at Killington on weekends; she was definitely a much better skier than I was. We used to have sex almost every day after school at her house, before her mother came home from work. Jerry used to say to me that there was nothing wrong with sex, as long as it is not abusive. She felt it was a way of uniting yourself with another being and experiencing their soul, along with their body. Maybe it was part of her Christian Science thing. I don't know if I was really into her soul, but I was definitely into her body. She was the most beautiful girl in high school.

"I could never quite figure out what she saw in me. I mean, she could have dated anybody. She was the prom queen type, she got straight A's in everything, plus she was just a really nice human being.

"I spent most of my time hanging around with the black and Hispanic kids in my school. They made more sense to me than most of the white kids did; we related to the same kinds of music and musicians: Santana, Miles Davis, John Coltrane, Jimi Hendrix, guys like that. My black friends used to take me with them to see Miles Davis and other great jazz and blues musicians play. I usually ended up being the token white person in these clubs, but I didn't care, I just got so high listening to the music! My black friends watched my back, so it was cool."

"Whatever happened to Jerry? Is she at home in America waiting for you?"

"No, we broke up. We went out together throughout high school, and she wanted to keep the relationship going. I think she really loved me. But I was a classic fuckup. I used to spend more time in the principal's office than in class. I used to have this problem with authority. I mean, I really don't like people telling me what to do, particularly when they're wrong.

"We graduated from high school, and Jerry went on to Harvard. I didn't want to go to college right away. I was burned out on school, and it really bored me. I sensed that there was a big world out there, and I wanted to experience it right away.

"I wasn't a total screwup, at least not academically," I said in defense of myself. "In high school I did well in things that I liked. I always got A's in English, science, and music. I really liked shop, too. I liked making things with my hands. But if a course bored me, or if the teacher had a condescending attitude, I would just totally flake out and do minimal work. I would cut classes, get detention . . . that sort of thing.

"My family really wanted me to go to college, but I didn't want to. I wanted to take a break and figure out what I wanted to do with my life first. They got really heavy about it, so I went for one semester, just to make them happy, but then I dropped out. I told them that I might go back later, but first I wanted to travel and see the world.

"As you might expect, Jerry wasn't too thrilled by my decision. She was already into thinking about getting married and what china patterns she was going to pick out. Bottom line? She was probably too good for me. I knew that. I just wasn't as good a person as she was. She worked harder and seemed to have a spiritual side to her that I lacked.

"I just had to go and experience the world. She cried and we talked about it a lot. I felt really bad for her. I don't know if I loved her, I mean, not in the same way that she loved me. But I did care for her. It was really hard.

"I told her that she could come with me if she wanted to. But she said that she wanted to go to Harvard and study archaeology. It was her thing, and I knew that she would be better off without me.

"What kind of a person am I? I just do what I want to. I'm into extreme athletics, Dostoevski, and martial arts, and I am just freaked out about taking on responsibilities. I want to be free, that's all.

"Marriage and children are just not me. I want to experience life completely, not just go through the motions like most people do. I can't imagine myself in a straight nine-to-five job. I'd go nuts! I mean, most people seem dead to me. It's like they're walking around and they're totally numb to the incredible beauty of life. They just knuckle under to authority, without questioning whether that authority is right or wrong."

"Do you think that you are better than most people, because you think this way?" Nadia asked, her tone softening slightly.

"No, not really. I feel that most people are better than I am.

I mean, I have had great coaches and teachers, and I know spiritual people like Jerry and Master Fwap. Obviously these people are more together than I am.

"I think the steady job is great for some people. But it's just not for me, at least not yet.

"Master Fwap told me that someday I was going to become enlightened and go back to college and get a Ph.D. He said I was going to become famous in the West and have a positive influence on millions of people. He told me that I would write books and music that would turn people on to higher consciousness, and also that I would really get into computers!

"I think Master Fwap is way off. Not about Buddhism—that's his thing, he definitely has his Buddhist monk act together—but he is way off the mark with me. I'm never going to do any of those things. I just want to snowboard the world. I want to see and experience that which is most beautiful while I'm alive and young, now, not when I'm sixty-five and retired in Florida or something.

"But getting back to your question, no, I don't think that I am better than other people. I mean, you're better than I am. You left Denmark to find enlightenment. You're like Jerry, you want to attain something higher in life. Me, I just want to have a good time. I'm just into living each day, one day at a time, for myself. I'm into rock and jazz, sports, and I read a lot of weird philosophy and science fiction.

"So no, Nadia, I'm not better than other people. I'm probably not as good as most people. I'm radical, that's all. I don't avoid trying new things because I am afraid of what other people will think of me, or because it hasn't been done before. Most people make the choices they do in life because they're afraid, afraid to deviate from what everyone else is doing around them.

"Whenever there is something that I am afraid of, I have to go and try it right away. Not something stupid, where I don't have a good chance of making it, but 'no fear' is definitely my motto."

"Do you have another girlfriend now?" Nadia asked, with a look of more than casual interest.

"No. I dated a bunch of other girls after Jerry, mainly sports types. But no one could ever measure up to her. I'm alone at the moment. What about yourself? Do you have a guy waiting for you back in Denmark? You must, you're too beautiful not to."

"Most men bore me. I have gone out with a lot of European men. They all think that a woman is a plaything, a possession. They do not interest me. No, there is no one special. I have never met a man who had real spiritual qualities. All the men I have known have been selfish. That is one of the reasons why I became interested in yoga. I was bored with men. Sex is good, but the men I have it with are, how would you say it in America, only into themselves? Is that right?"

"Yes, that's the way we say it."

There was a short silence, and then Nadia continued, "For now I am looking for enlightenment. I know I was enlightened before, a monk I met in Cambodia told me this. He was very old and very wise. When he said it, something in my heart made me know his words were true. I asked him if I could study with him, but he said no, that I had to travel and find another master. He was not the karmically correct master for me. So, here I am in Nepal, looking but not yet finding. It is ironic, no?"

"Yes, it is," I said with a yawn. I suddenly realized how tired I was. As entranced as I was by Nadia's radiant beauty, I was having trouble keeping my eyes open. I put my head down on the pillow and closed my eyes.

"You are so tired," Nadia said in a soft and gentle voice.

I mumbled something to her about traveling a long way on foot over high passes just to meet her. The next thing I knew she was sitting next to me on my bed.

"Take off your shirt and I will rub your shoulders, then you will feel better. I studied massage for a while. Now take off your shirt," she said in a no-nonsense tone of voice.

"But Nadia," I murmured, "I don't know if we should do this here. I mean, it's not exactly private."

"No one else is in the room but us. The rest have all gone out drinking. Don't be so embarrassed, we are all alone. You are not afraid of me, are you? I thought you said that your motto was 'no fear.'"

"No, I'm not afraid of you. I'm just exhausted."

I was so tired I didn't even know what I was doing. I managed to get my shirt off, and then I lay on my bunk on my stomach, with my face half buried in my pillow. Nadia's smooth, cool hands started to rub my shoulders gently. I fell asleep in about thirty seconds.

I awoke several hours later, and the lights in the hostel dormitory had been turned off. I heard the gentle sound of someone breathing next to me. It was Nadia. She had curled up beside me in my bed and fallen asleep.

She had covered us both up with one of the thick, coarse woolen hostel blankets. I was afraid to move because I didn't want to awaken her. Her breathing was very slow and rhythmic. I was still pretty groggy, but I could distinctly feel the heat from her body warming me.

Her skin was against mine. It took me a second to dope out that she had taken all her clothes off and was lying naked next to me.

I still had my pants and socks on. I was unsure what to do, so I just lay in bed listening to her breathe, feeling her soft skin against my chest, staring up into the darkness above us.

Then she rolled over toward me and put her left arm around my waist, mumbling something in Danish. It appeared she was talking in her sleep.

Lying next to her naked body in the darkness, listening to her soft breathing, I began to get very turned on. I thought about touching her, but I didn't know if it would offend her. I knew that Danish people were much more comfortable with nudity than Americans, so her taking her clothes off wasn't necessarily an invitation to have sex with her. So I did nothing. I just lay there and wondered how Master Fwap could always be so right about everything.

After lying there for a while Nadia suddenly woke up. She yawned and then put both her arms around me, pulling me close to her.

My heart began to pound. I put my arms around her and held her. We lay like that for a long time, not talking, just holding on to each other, listening to the cold gusts of wind blowing down the streets of Katmandu in the depths of the Nepalese night.

Nadia moved her right leg gently between my legs and then curled herself around me. Then she softly laughed. She must have felt the fact that I was very turned on and also undecided as to what course of action I should take.

"Take off your pants," she whispered in a soft, seductive voice. "I think you will find it much easier to have sex with me without them on."

62

Without any hesitation, I immediately complied with her request. We pressed our naked bodies against each other, lying side by side.

Our mouths found each other and we began to kiss, first slowly on the lips, and then with our tongues. Kissing Nadia felt very different from any other woman I had ever kissed before: it was both more sensual, and at the same time less physical. I felt like I was meditating.

As we continued kissing deeply, in addition to sensing the softness and strength of her body and her musky smell, I could feel her inside my mind. I wasn't thinking, only feeling.

Normally, when I have sex with a woman I always think a lot. I think about what to do next, analyze how I feel, or sometimes my mind drifts away to topics that have nothing to do with the sexual activity I'm participating in. With Nadia, sex was completely different. My mind was silent, just as it was when I meditated with Master Fwap or when I do my best snowboarding.

She reached her hand out and began to touch my genitals. I was already hard as a rock, and the soft motion of her hand on my penis sent waves of ecstasy through me. I placed my hand gently on her vagina, and she was very wet.

I brought my mouth down and began to kiss and lick her right breast and nipple. She moaned again, this time more deeply, and pushed me toward the edge of the small bed and pulled me on top of her.

I raised my body to make it easier for her, and then, after motionlessly lying on top of her for several minutes, I kissed her again, this time with much greater intensity.

She reached for me, and I slid it into her. Moaning very softly, she began slowly moving back and forth.

Then a very weird thing happened. The room went white. At

63

first I thought that someone had turned on the lights, then I realized that I was seeing Nadia's aura. It was pale white, the color of the moonlight against the fresh Himalayan snow. We were both moving harder against each other now.

I put both of my hands down underneath her, and she lifted her legs slightly, bending them at the knees. Her musky smell was stronger now than before. As she put her tongue inside my ear, her body began to move faster against mine. As I slid in and out of her, there was a feeling of perfect motion between us. We moved together in a way that I have never experienced before or since, with any other woman.

I felt somewhat dissociated by the bright whiteness of her aura and also by the fact that I wasn't thinking. In a strange but not unpleasant way, I felt very removed from the sexual activities that Nadia and I were sharing.

She tightened her thighs against me, keeping our movements closer together. I was feeling wonderful, but I could sense by the motion of her body that she was hitting higher levels of ecstatic pleasure than I was.

Then she came. Her body shook convulsively under mine, but she didn't make a sound.

While I was still indulging in the sense of nonreality of the entire experience I was having with Nadia, she whispered in my ear, "You must come now too. You don't have to wait."

It hit me then that I didn't really care whether I had an orgasm. I was so high on her energy that the entire idea of having an orgasm seemed inconsequential. Never being one to argue with a beautiful woman, I started to drill down to the sensations of my physical body. It took a couple of minutes for me to get fully back into my body, but then my sexual experience with Nadia took off.

I felt the soft hardness of her body completely, which was

punctuated by a pulsing, tingling energy that I felt when I entered her more deeply. The pulsing energy inside her body wasn't physical, though, it was more like the waves of intense Kundalini energy I have experienced while meditating with Master Fwap.

I then experimented with moving my body against Nadia's body in different ways. By focusing on her energy, and moving my body in harmony with it, her energy became even stronger. Nadia was starting to get turned on again.

She started to perspire more when my movements synchronized with the energy I was feeling inside her. She had another orgasm. This time her body shook even more strongly than before, but still she didn't make a sound.

Finally I came. It was definitely anticlimactic; I hardly felt it. But she did. She moaned, kissed me, and held me closely to her. We lay together with our arms wrapped around each other for a long time.

Afterward, we turned on our sides, facing each other. She wrapped her legs around me and kissed me again. She put her tongue deep inside of my mouth, moving it gently, probing ever more deeply into my mouth.

Then it was over. I pulled my arms back from around her, and in a few minutes I drifted back off to sleep.

Master Fwap and the Oracle were talking to me. I was trying to figure out what they were saying, but I couldn't quite make it out. I was up on the top of a snow-covered Himalayan peak with Master Fwap and the Oracle, standing on my jet-black snowboard, getting ready to make a run down the mountain.

"I'm dreaming!" I thought to myself. "This is just a dream."

"That's right," Master Fwap chimed in. "Isn't he clever?" Master Fwap laughed, gesturing to the Oracle. Then they both began to laugh.

"We told you that you were going to get close to her. How was it?" Master Fwap said with a chuckle. Before I could say anything, both he and the Oracle started to howl with laughter.

"Now wait a minute, isn't anything private around here?" I asked them.

"Absolutely not," replied the Oracle. "How can anything be private when we are all telepathic? And why should it be? You didn't do anything wrong, you know; she loves you, even though she isn't fully consciously aware of that yet. Is the Catholic Church getting the better of you again? Do you feel guilty? Is sex something you have to do in the dark and hide?"

"In Tantric Buddhism we feel that everything is holy," Master Fwap added. "We believe that all heavens and hells are created inside of your own mind, by your own thoughts. If your thoughts are pure and innocent, then no matter what you do physically, you will live in psychic heaven, but if your thoughts are filled with violence and deception, then no matter how pure your outer experiences may appear, you will live in the spiritual hell of your own mind."

The Oracle chimed in, "Was it as good for you as it was for her?"

"Now wait a minute. That wasn't normal sex, and she's not a normal woman. I could see her aura, and there was a lot of energy running back and forth between our bodies that wasn't sexual. It was powerful, but it wasn't very physical."

"Maybe not for you, but it certainly was for her," Master Fwap stated factually.

"Perhaps you got a little too high on her energy and missed the best part," the Oracle added.

"But Master Fwap, I couldn't do anything else. It was hard to be physical with her. What am I supposed to be with her? I thought that you guys were Buddhist monks, and you're teaching me how to get away from physical pleasure and to be spiritual instead," I shot back at them, in a complaining tone of voice.

"No, not at all," Master Fwap gently responded. "You're missing the point: Samsara is nirvana. From the Tantric Buddhist point of view, there isn't a difference between that which is physical and that which is spiritual, unless you create that difference with your own impure thoughts."

"I'm confused."

"So is most of the world," responded the Oracle. "What does that have to do with anything?"

"Isn't enlightenment supposed to put an end to confusion?" I asked hesitantly.

"Yes, of course it is," Master Fwap said. "But you are not enlightened, nor is the world, so of course you are confused."

"Well, I thought Buddhist monks were supposed to help unconfuse unenlightened types like myself."

"Confusion is a necessary first step on the pathway to enlightenment," Master Fwap began. "Look at it from our point of view for a moment. You just made love to a beautiful woman, had your first transcendental sexual experience, and now you want to be instantly enlightened about everything. Don't you think you might be rushing things just a little bit? Most of the deeper truths of eternity take many incarnations to understand. Why don't you just enjoy your time with your Danish friend, and then, when you are ready and your power is up, come with us to the Anapurna range. You still have an important riddle to solve, or have you forgotten about that already?"

"So what am I supposed to do with Nadia? She doesn't snowboard, and she is looking for an enlightened teacher. Should I bring her along with me on our journey?"

"No, she has other karmic experiences to go through. It is your karma to come with us. Don't forget the dimensions," responded the Oracle.

"Now why don't you stop asking so many questions and snowboard down the mountain," Master Fwap instructed me. "Make your mind empty, and let the mountain's second attention guide you. Remember, you are the board; do not allow a mental separation to occur between yourself and your snowboard. Feel that your snowboard is animate, that it is alive, and allow your two energies to perfectly merge. Now, let's see if you can turn snowboarding into proper Buddhist practice."

With that, I pushed off and started to carve in and out of the mountain's granular powder. I did a major spinning jump off a sharp vertical slope, and was just about to touch down, when my dream abruptly ended.

6

A Tale of Two Snowboards

When I awoke, Nadia was nowhere to be found, and the hostel dormitory was deserted. I had obviously overslept. Immediately I got up and, after hitting the washroom, decided to go snowboarding.

While I was dressing as fast as I could, not wanting to miss any more of the day than I already had, a most unusual thing happened to me: I couldn't make up my mind whether to take my long or short snowboard up to the mountains with me.

Normally, when I'm heading off to go snowboarding, I have a gut feeling as to whether I want to take my long board (which is better suited for carving and cutting in deep powder) or my short board (which is excellent for extreme vertical terrain and high jumps). But today, for some unfathomable reason, I felt ambivalent about which board to bring. Master Fwap probably would have said that I was totally out of touch with my second attention.

I finally ended my mental conflict by taking both boards with me, assuming that once I got to the mountain, I would assess the snow and terrain conditions, pick the appropriate board, strap my second board underneath my day pack, and snowboard down the mountain with my second board attached to my back—something I had never tried before.

It was around ten o'clock when I left the hostel. Fortunately, I quickly managed to hitch a ride with a group of Japanese mountain climbers who were headed for the backcountry in their beat-up Land Rover.

They dropped me at the top of a fourteen-thousand-foot pass—which is as high as the road went—and I spent the next several hours trudging up another three thousand feet to the top of the peak.

I adjust to altitude shifts very quickly, but even so, every thousand feet above fourteen thousand that day required an extreme effort on my part, causing me to climb more slowly than usual.

All of the snowboarding I had done thus far in the Himalayas had ranged from fourteen to nineteen thousand feet. Beyond nineteen thousand feet, a gradual altitude adjustment by staying at base camps would really be required, unless of course I was a snowboarding sherpa or had a helicopter.

I certainly didn't have the money to charter a helicopter, and since most of the choppers in the area were either military or reserved for mountain rescue, climbing up the snow- and ice-covered face of the mountain that day was my fate. Master Fwap had once told me that the exercise of climbing the mountains before I snowboarded down them was good for me and that it would help me to develop character. Not!

After reaching the top of the peak, I began to prepare to snowboard down. The slope was relatively vertical and gnarly, so I decided to use my short board. I was just about to strap my long board onto my back and hook my day pack over it, when I heard a voice humming a Buddhist chant behind me.

I slowly turned around, expecting to see nothing. I figured I was simply hearing the voice of the disembodied master I had heard on my last solo snowboarding adventure. But much to my amazement, Master Fwap was standing directly behind me, his ocher monk's robe gently fluttering in the Himalayan mountain breeze.

"Master Fwap! What are you doing up here?"

"I have come to give you a lesson in Tantric snowboarding. I am glad that you had the courtesy to bring a snowboard along for my use," he continued. "That was very Buddhist of you."

"Master Fwap, in all honesty, I brought both boards up here today because I didn't know which one I wanted to use. I really didn't anticipate meeting you up here."

"Ah, but your second attention—the deeper part of your being—obviously knew that you and I were going to encounter each other here; it also knew that I would require the use of one of your two snowboards. Remember, your conscious mind is aware of only a small portion of reality, but the nonphysical portion of your mind, which I refer to as the second attention, is aware of things your conscious mind can't even begin to fathom."

"How can that be? If that is the case, why doesn't my second attention always prepare me for whatever is going to happen to me each day of my life?"

"Why don't we sit down on your snowboards for a few minutes," he suggested, "and I will explain."

I set my long board down on the white snow in front of Master Fwap and took a seat to the right of him on my short board. Master Fwap gracefully seated himself on my long board, sitting in a cross-legged position, carefully folding his robe under his knees.

"You are familiar with icebergs, yes?" I nodded.

"Well, when you see an iceberg floating in the water, I am sure that you are also aware that at least two-thirds of its mass exists under water and is invisible to your eyes. Try to imagine that the human mind is like an iceberg," he continued, slightly shifting his position on my snowboard. "The conscious minds of people who do not practice meditation, as you now do, are simply not in touch with most of reality. They do not realize, as you are just beginning to, that most of existence lies on the other side of consciousness, veiled by their thoughts and ideas. As a matter of fact, most are in touch only with a tiny segment of their mind's totality."

"Are you referring to what Western psychologists call the subconscious mind?"

"No, not at all," he said in a dismissive tone of voice. "Your subconscious mind is a portion of your physical brain; it is composed of neurological cell structures. I am referring to your second attention, which is the nonphysical portion of your mind.

"As I have told you before," Master Fwap reminded me, "your second attention is your spiritual body. It is composed of two sections, your astral body and your causal body. Your astral body gives you access to the various astral dimensions, and your causal body gives you the ability to merge with the higher causal dimensions of light that exist in the highest planes of consciousness.

"Most human beings are completely oblivious to the astral and causal portions of their minds. It is in and through the regular practices of meditation and mindfulness that a person can gradually awaken and forge a link between the conscious mind and the second attention. It takes many years of meditation and mindfulness to gain full access to your second attention," Master Fwap said, assuming the tone of voice he used when he discoursed on complicated Buddhist subjects.

"As you are currently observing, having practiced meditation and mindfulness for little more than a month has already given you some access to your second attention. The proof of this is that your second attention knew you were going to encounter me on the top of this mountain today—even though your conscious mind was oblivious to this fact—and caused you to bring both of your snowboards up here with you, because it knew that I would require the use of one of them."

"But how can this be?"

"Why does the sun rise in the sky in the east every morning? Why do birds fly through the air? Why do the seasons revolve in perfect harmony? Buddhist masters do not have answers to the 'whys' of life; that is for philosophers to debate. But what we do know is that life is much more mysterious, complicated, and beautiful than most people suppose.

"In Buddhism," he continued to explain, "we simply accept that things exist in the universe the way that they do, because they do. Through the study and practice of Buddhist yoga, masters gradually come to understand both the surface and the depths of life, and then divine how this information can take them and others beyond the shores of pain, across the seas of mental, emotional, and spiritual suffering and death—to the land of eternal ecstasy and immortal light.

"Now that I have taught you something about Buddhism, it is your turn to teach me something," Master Fwap said, addressing me in a less serious tone of voice.

"What can I possibly teach you, Master Fwap? You know everything about everything. You can even snowboard better than I can. I still can't believe how you managed that! I mean, you had never been on a snowboard before, and I saw you not only snowboard perfectly down a mountain that would be difficult for an expert snowboarder, but you then somehow managed to levitate both yourself and my snowboard back up to the top of the mountain. How can I possibly teach you anything?"

Master Fwap looked at me with an expression that I can only characterize as youthful. Suddenly his facial expression instantly transformed from that of an aged and formal Buddhist monk to that of a youngster excited about learning something new. I didn't know if he was mimicking the way I looked at him when I asked him questions, or whether this was a side of his personality I had not witnessed before.

"Tell me about this sport of yours, snowboarding. How did it begin, and why did you become involved in it?"

"Well," I began, "snowboarding really started to happen in the 1960s with the invention of the Snurfer. There was this guy named Sherman Poppen. He came up with a radical piece of winter sports equipment that looked something like a single water ski without any bindings. It had a clunky handle that was attached to a rope that was hooked to the front of the thing. And there was a traction pad fastened to the board that helped keep your feet from sliding off. It was kind of like a weird megatoboggan thing that you stood on as you went zooming down a snow-covered mountain, holding onto the handle for dear life. Poppen was a great inventor, and I guess it just made sense from his point of view to surf frozen water on mountains as well as regular waves in the ocean.

"Snurfers then got picked up by an outfit called Brunswick Sporting Goods and sold for around twenty dollars. The Snurfers eventually evolved into snowboards. Two brothers, Jake Burton and Steve Burton Carpenter, took the Snurfer concept—which was coming out of the surfing world—and because they were both skiers and Snurfer freaks, they started modifying the concept. Steve was an expert in fiberglass and resins, Jake added rubber straps to the board to help stabilize it, and their designs just kept getting better and better. Also Jake really saw that the sport was going to go worldwide; he has probably done more good PR for snowboarding than anyone else on the planet.

"Around this time, other people were starting to develop snow-

74

boards. On the West Coast, Tom Sims, an ultraskateboarder, had gotten into building snowboards, and in New York, Dimitrije Milovichm, an engineering dude, was making epoxy and fiber boards, which he started selling through his company, Winter Stick.

"Things just took off from there, and people started to ride high. Chuck Barfoot, Chris Sanders, and other early pioneers of the sport started to refine riding techniques. Better and better bindings and snowboarding boots came in . . . we had a new sport!

"The thing to understand about snowboarding," I said didactically, "is that it is a lot of different things to a lot of different people. From my point of view, it is definitely more radical than skiing with your mother and father on weekends.

"There are basically three different schools of snowboarding," I continued, in my newfound role as snowboarding guru. "You have your skateboarder crossovers, the kids who do half pipe and way cool trick riding; you have your skier crossovers, who are usually slightly older types who have brought the style and grace of alpine skiing to snowboarding; and then you have your surfer crossovers, who are more into what I would call the 'spiritual' side of snowboarding.

"Your skier crossovers are mainly into altitude and deep-powder boarding. Since they are already masters of the skiing scene, they are very comfortable with altitude and long jumps. But your surfer crossovers are coming from a whole different place. To really understand where they are coming from, you have got to get into the whole surfer mentality.

"Surfing is a sport that requires a very heavy commitment," I continued, leaning slightly forward on my board. "Normally, when you surf, you get up at dawn and you ride waves, and then you return in the late afternoon—after working all day—when the surf's up, and catch the late afternoon swells. While there are competitions, it is really not a competitive sport. You spend a lot of time hanging out on your board in the water, waiting for the perfect wave to break. Surfing definitely attracts both a more dedicated and laid-back crowd than most other sports.

"Also," I continued, hoping I wasn't either losing or boring Master Fwap, "the balance and patience factors are much more critical in surfing than they are in snowboarding, as is the danger factor. If you're out surfing serious waves and you wipe out, you don't land on soft snow. It's usually either very sharp coral, or you get raked across the beach gravel and sand while you're tumbling underwater.

"Then, there is the whole snowboarding image thing. The skateboarder crossovers helped give the 'bad boy' image to snowboarding. While they are amazing riders, some of them tend to be a little bit rude and party heavily. I skateboard a little myself, but it's not really my main thing. I'm mostly coming from the surfing side, with some alpine techniques that I picked up skiing and a little bit of the 'no fear' attitude I got into when I was skateboarding.

"For me," I continued, "snowboarding is mostly like surfing. I'm into extreme vertical and off-piste boarding. I like to ride alone, otherwise I find myself competing with the guys around me, and that's not what it's all about for me. It's not about winning or losing, it's about just doing it. The only person I'm competing with when I go snowboarding is myself.

"I have total respect for all other snowboarders and their styles, except, of course, for the macho, out-of-control types. They are the ones who are really starting to give the sport a raunchy reputation. I like to drink a couple of beers with friends at a club after a day of major boarding or surfing, too, but the actual experience of snowboarding and surfing is more of a transcendental thing for me. That's the only way I can describe it.

"I love the athletic challenge," I continued on enthusiastically, "and being in nature, but I think the numero uno reason I am into surfing and snowboarding is that it takes me to a really clean place inside my head. I guess it's my way of meditating."

"I have heard you use two terms, 'carving' and 'cutting,'" Master Fwap interjected. "What is the difference between them?"

"Snowboarding is really developing a new vocabulary. There are hardly any words for what we are doing yet. So everybody in the sport seems to have his or her own terminology. Let me answer your question by first explaining the four different types of riding: alpine, free riding, freestyle, and extreme snowboarding.

"Alpine snowboarding, as I mentioned to you a few minutes ago, comes mainly from your skier crossovers. It involves mostly carving, which are gentle sloping turns where the edge of your snowboard is literally carving into the packed snow. When you carve properly, your turns are caused by gradual weight and stance shifts that you make on your board.

"Free riding has evolved mainly from your skateboarder crossovers. It involves trick riding, major jumps, and half pipe. Most of the kids like free riding.

"Freestyle is a mixture of both free riding and alpine, only it's a lot more intense. It's for riders who really want to push their limits.

"Extreme snowboarding is mainly about boarding heavy vertical drops. It's the most dangerous type of riding and definitely not for beginners. It's usually done off-piste, meaning in the backcountry, away from regular runs and lifts. That's where cutting comes into play. Cutting is radical carving, only you can't ride your edges too deeply into the snow or you will flip."

"Why is it more dangerous?" Master Fwap asked. "I would think jumping would be."

"Not really. I mean, not really unless you're a bad free rider. Jumping is very smooth, unless you are doing a lot of double spins or flips. The impact on landing is mostly absorbed by your board and heavily cushioned by the snow you're landing on. Naturally, you have to line up your angles correctly on an extreme jump, or you and the ski patrol are going to go on a toboggan ride down the mountain together.

"The real danger in extreme snowboarding comes in a bunch of forms: falls, avalanches, ice, altitude, rapid weather changes, rocks, crevasses, and unknown terrain. You've got to be able to deal with spending time at high altitudes, and some people just can't. I have never had a problem with altitude sickness, but I know a lot of people who have. I think it's because I did so much long-distance running and swimming in high school, or maybe it's just genetic or something. I can normally adjust from fourteen to nineteen thousand feet without a major hassle.

"Now, a lot of high-altitude snowboarders have to do the base camp thing, like in mountain climbing. They get up to about sixteen thousand feet and camp there for a couple of days to acclimatize to the thinner air. I don't find that necessary, although if I started going over nineteen thousand feet, I'm sure I would.

"Also, when you are dealing with higher-altitude snowboarding, it's colder, and the weather and temperature can change much faster than at lower altitudes. A fast weather change or temperature drop, combined with a lack of oxygen, can completely throw off your balance and visual perception.

"The greatest danger in extreme snowboarding is avalanches. So it is imperative that an extreme or off-piste snowboarder learn the signs for detecting potential avalanche situations. If you get caught in an avalanche, then it's *adios muchachos*."

"How can you tell if you are in avalanche territory?" Master Fwap asked with a concerned look on his face.

"Well, aside from a gut feeling, which you would probably refer to as a message from my second attention, I consider all of the standard observable factors, but it is also helpful to understand what causes avalanches to happen in the first place. Avalanches are caused by the layering of snow. When snow falls in a storm, it creates a layer. Every additional storm adds another layer. As long as all of the layers fall and remain at about the same temperature, there is actually very little danger of an avalanche. But if you have a lot of different layers of snow that are at different temperatures, you have a high avalanche probability. About eighty-five percent of all avalanches occur within twenty-four hours of a new snowstorm.

"Aside from being wary of new snow and checking with the local authorities about potential avalanche conditions," I continued to explain, "I like to observe a few things firsthand, with my own eyes and other senses. For example, if the snow feels empty or hollow when you are walking on it, you have weakly packed snow. If I see a lot of snow runoff, that tells me that the pack isn't tight yet. Heavy wind conditions and extreme snow rates are also tip-offs; if you're dealing with a snow rate of more than two inches an hour for five or six hours, it's prudent to rethink your ride. Also, if you have several hours of heavy winds, the drifts that accumulate can create serious avalanche potential.

"It's also not a bad idea to dig snow pits to see how the snowpack is layered. I always advise anyone new to backcountry snowboarding first to take a course in avalanche detection and rescue before attempting radical boarding. Being buried alive under tons of snow that is moving at over a hundred miles an hour is not my idea of a peak snowboarding experience.

"Then there are the other usual problems that are related to extreme vertical snowboarding. Normally when you start your run, you're on top of a peak. The windchill factors are higher, and it's easy to get frostbite without realizing it. You're also dealing with more rocks higher up, because the snowpack is usually lighter. So what looks like a pile of snow can really be a rock with just a light glaze of snow covering it.

"In extreme snowboarding, you also tend to run into more ice because of the cold. Ice is one of the snowboarder's worst enemies. It's very hard to control your board on ice. The hairiest thing that you can encounter in extreme snowboarding are crevasses. Falling into a crevasse is bad for your board and worse for your bod. I had a good friend who died boarding into a crevasse—they never even found his body.

"The final dangers," I said in summation, "are falls and unknown terrain. It's one thing to fall on a standard trail, but if you do an extreme vertical drop-fall, you are definitely going to break bones. In addition, it's very easy to get lost off-piste, so it's important to carry a compass, map out where you are going, and always have a good sense of your bearings."

"This all makes sense," Master Fwap replied in a judicious tone of voice, "but one thing I still don't fully understand is your ability to deal with altitudes so easily. Living in the Himalayas acclimatizes the sherpas and mountain guides to constant altitude changes, but you also spend a lot of time at sea level."

"Master Fwap, I trained for snowboarding. Before I came over here, I was snowboarding in the American and Canadian Rocky Mountains for months. I can jog at fourteen thousand feet. So, while fifteen to nineteen thousand feet is certainly challenging, when I go boarding at those altitudes, I am in top shape. Even my low-altitude workout schedule is pretty intense. Some people can just tolerate high-altitude snowboarding and mountain climbing, while other people can't.

"I watch myself constantly for the usual signs of altitude sickness," I continued in response, "and if I see any of them, I immediately snowboard down the mountain, rest, drink lots of fluids, and take a few days off. In Boulder, where I like to spend some time mountain climbing each summer, I have met a lot of mountain climbers who can tolerate much higher altitude changes than I can, with even less preparation.

"I've asked some of them about it, and their answer was that the more altitude work you do, the faster you readjust. That's been my experience, too. When I first started at fourteen and fifteen thousand feet, I thought I would never be able to go higher. But the more I did it, the easier it got. I really don't see a future for myself snowboarding above nineteen thousand feet. I'm sure that there are people who will do it with helicopters, base camps, and all that stuff. But for me, that is all too much of a hassle.

"If I have to go through all of that just to make a run, why bother? For me, the beauty of snowboarding is that I can be alone in perfect powder, challenging myself both physically and mentally, and I can push back my fear limits to the max. I like the adrenaline rush of extreme boarding, but I also do a fair amount of lower-altitude freestyle boarding, just because it is so beautiful."

We sat in silence for several minutes after I had finished. All around us the snow-covered mountains provided one of the most beautiful panoramic vistas of the Himalayas I had yet seen. Then, quite suddenly, Master Fwap stood up and instructed me with his left hand to do the same.

"Now it is time to try snowboarding together. I will lead and you will follow. See if you can keep up with me," Master Fwap said with a grin on his face.

As we mounted our boards, I snapped my snowboarding boots into their bindings, but Master Fwap just stood on his board in his monk's boots, between the bindings, ignoring them. He intended to ride his snowboard without bindings, as if it were a surfboard.

Master Fwap pushed off and started down. The first few hundred meters were extreme vertical, and then the slope evened off into waves of powder on what I still considered to be a heady incline.

Masterfully cutting in and out of the vertical drop, Master Fwap began to carve back and forth in the granular powder as it started to even out partway down the slope.

Pushing off, I did some fast cuts and a high jump. It went well and I did a razor-back landing on the soft powder below. Then I started carving tightly, following Master Fwap's snowboarding trail for direction.

I snowboarded as fast as I could, but no matter what I did, I was unable to keep up with Master Fwap. The faster I moved, the farther ahead of me he got, until I completely lost sight of him.

Following his tracks down to the bottom of the mountain, I found him standing waiting for me. He laughed with glee for a minute or two, and I must have had a pretty amazed look on my face.

"Why isn't snowboarding an Olympic sport, like skiing?"

"Most snowboarders have a bad reputation, Master Fwap. It's an antiestablishment kind of sport. I don't think they would ever let snowboarders into the Olympics. The skiers don't like us, to begin with, and it's just not popular enough. I mean, for a sport to go Olympic, you need sponsors and all kinds of things."

"Before we begin our journey back to Katmandu, I have a

prophecy for you," Master Fwap said in a serious tone of voice. "One day this sport of yours will be more popular than skiing. It will capture the imagination of the world, and yes, one day it will be an Olympic event."

"No way, Master Fwap, no offense intended."

"None taken, but stranger things have happened."

"Yes, but why would anyone care about a bunch of low-life snowboarders. It's more likely that surfing will become an Olympic sport. It's been around long enough, there are lots of competitions, and there are major board companies that would sponsor it."

"The future is unknown," Master Fwap replied mysteriously, with a twinkle in his eyes, "but that is my prophecy nevertheless. Only time will tell if I am correct or incorrect."

We stopped talking after that. I shouldered both of my boards and day pack, and the two of us began the trek down to the road. We hitched a ride back to Katmandu in an old beat-up army truck that was filled with hippies who had come to Nepal looking for Ram Dass.

7

Chaos Theory and Virtual
Avalanches

We arrived back in Katmandu shortly after sunset. After disembarking from the army truck, whose riders' conversations on the way back had mostly revolved around local hashish prices, Master Fwap and I parted. I returned to the hostel in search of Nadia, and Master Fwap went back to his temple.

I found Nadia sitting in the kitchen, helping a few of our fellow hostelmates prepare dinner. Tonight was stew and bread night. There were seven of us at the dinner table. After finishing our meal and cleaning up, Nadia and I both retired to the dormitory.

She seemed much happier and also even more beautiful than I had remembered her to be, from our brief but intense encounter the night before. She was wearing a short aquamarine dress, black hose, a white zippered top, and black cotton slippers. She had on light blue glitter nail polish that matched her dress, and she was wearing a soft shade of pink lipstick. She looked very hip and appealing, and I felt like having sex with her immediately.

Instead of letting her hair down that evening, she had braided it into a knot behind her head. Sitting next to her in her Eurotech getup, it hit me that I must have looked pretty disheveled after a day of mountain climbing and snowboarding so I excused myself and went and took a freezing cold shower, since no hot water was available. I then shaved, put on some clean jeans, my best-looking sweatshirt, and thermal socks and started preparing myself for another potential intimate encounter with her.

Returning to the dorm after my shower, I found Nadia sitting on her bed reading. I quietly approached, sat down next to her on my bed, and said nothing. I sensed that I shouldn't come on too strong, so I took *The Handbook for Enlightenment* out of my day pack. I thought if she saw me reading a Buddhist text, it might enhance her opinion of me and increase my possibilities of another intimate encounter.

After thumbing through the book for a few seconds, I found the opening page of the second chapter and began to read.

Meditation is a practice that involves slowing and eventually stopping your thought process. Within you is infinite light, power, and ecstasy. But just as sunlight is blocked out by the clouds, your own thoughts block your access to the endless realities that exist within your higher mind.

Success in meditation depends on right practices, consistency, and—if possible—regular empowerments by a Tantric root guru.

Right practices are the basic, intermediate, and advanced secret meditation techniques, coupled with the continual practice of mindfulness.

Consistency means that it is necessary for you to practice meditation twice a day without fail. This practice demands your full conscious attention during your meditation sessions and should not degenerate into daydreaming.

Empowerments by your Tantric root guru will speed your progress significantly. A root guru has the ability to transfer different types of Kundalini energy into your consciousness. This energy will make it much easier for you to clear your mind and focus during your meditation periods, thus affording you much faster progress along the pathway to enlightenment.

THE PRELIMINARY PRACTICES

Meditation should be practiced in a clean place, either in- or out-of-doors, depending on your circumstances. It is recommended that you sit in a cross-legged position, keeping your spine straight. Most people find that sitting on a small meditation rug or cushion makes their meditation experience more comfortable and consequently they are less distracted by their physical body.

The goal in meditation is the complete cessation of all thought during the period you have set aside for meditation. This will take some time for most of you to achieve.

In the beginning, it is advised that you practice meditation while focusing on a physical or mental image, in order to help you to gradually develop your concentration skills. Once you have developed your concentration skills to a high degree, you will find it relatively effortless to slip into a state of meditative emptiness.

Initially, when you first begin the practice of meditation, don't fight with your thoughts or try to suppress them with your will. This will only frustrate you and bind you to your thoughts even more strongly. Instead, spend your time concentrating on your visualization or focusing on a mantra or a yantra.

For the first three months of practice, spend about fifteen minutes meditating twice a day. After about three months of consistent practice, increase your time to thirty minutes. After six months of consistent practice, increase your session time to forty-five minutes. After a year of practice, increase your session time to one hour, twice daily.

Once you have reached this time level, it is not really necessary to add more time to your meditation practice. Instead, what becomes of paramount importance is to decrease your thought flow during your sessions. When you can successfully meditate for two hours a day, with few—if any—thoughts, you will be ready for the advanced secret meditation techniques.

The best times of day to meditate are in the morning, during the period of sunset, or before going to sleep. Meditating in the morning clears your mind for the day ahead. It fills you with higher energy, so that you will have a happier and more creative day, and it also makes it easier for you to practice mindfulness during the day.

It is very easy to meditate at sunset. At that time a special doorway opens up between the interdimensional worlds, allowing you to meditate powerfully and also to recharge yourself with energy for the evening ahead.

If you cannot meditate at sunset, have your second meditation before going to sleep at night. You will find that you will sleep more peacefully and your mind will be clear and energized when you awaken the next morning.

Do not be discouraged! In the beginning of your practice you may feel like you are wasting your time. Initially, you may find it difficult to concentrate, and you will probably spend more time "thinking" about meditation and other topics than you will actually spend concentrating and meditating. This is quite normal.

Just keep practicing. Even after a few weeks you will begin to notice that your mind is much more clear, that you are happier, more aware, and have more physical, mental, and psychic energy. After several months of consistent practice, you will also notice that you require less sleep.

THE PRELIMINARY PRACTICES OF VISUALIZATION AND MANTRA YOGA

The following are a series of the secret basic and intermediate meditation techniques.

THE BLUE SKY

As you start your meditation, picture a beautiful blue sky without any clouds in it. As you picture the clear blue sky, feel that your body is growing lighter and lighter. Close your eyes and keep the image of the blue sky in your mind.

There are no limits to the blue sky. It stretches on endlessly in every direction, never beginning and never ending. As you visualize the blue sky, feel that your body has become so light that you have floated up into the clear blue sky. Visualize that you are floating in the sky, and that all tension, fatigue, worry, and problems have left you. Relax your mind and allow your breathing to seek its own level. Feel yourself floating gently in the clear blue sky that stretches endlessly in every direction, never beginning and never ending.

After several minutes have passed and you feel your thoughts slowing, picture that your entire body is merging with the blue sky. Your body is merging with the peace of the blue sky.... Your mind is merging with the tranquility of the blue sky.... Feel that you have actually become the blue sky. You no longer have a body or a mind. You have become the infinite blue sky that stretches endlessly in every direction, never beginning and never ending. Feel that you have become the perfect peace and tranquility of the blue sky. Completely let go and experience the bliss of meditation.

When you have completed your meditation session, open your eyes. You will now have a new and deeper sense of peace, relaxation, and poise. This renewed energy, joy, and calm will stay with you after you resume your normal activities.

THE TOWER OF LIGHT

Take a deep breath and exhale slowly. As you exhale, mentally picture all tiredness, tension, and fatigue leaving you. Then turn your attention to the crown of your head. Visualize that a wave of golden light is entering into you at the top of your head and passing throughout your entire body. Imagine this golden light passing from the crown of your head, through your neck, shoulders, arms, chest, stomach, lower back, and down your legs to your feet.

As you imagine the golden light passing throughout your body, feel yourself relaxing. Picture another wave of golden light entering through the crown of your head and visualize it passing through your entire body and then leaving through the soles of your feet. Feel that wave after wave of golden light is passing through you in this way. Each wave of golden light that passes through your body removes more of your tension, quiets your mind, and helps you to enter farther and deeper into a state of meditation.

Picture that the waves of golden light have now become a solid river of golden light that is constantly passing through you. Picture this golden light expanding beyond your body and filling up the entire room. Then visualize the golden light expanding beyond the earth ...beyond the sky...into the infinite. Feel that the golden light is constantly passing through you and washing all of your tensions, problems, and worries beyond you, beyond the earth...beyond the sky...and into the infinite. Continue visualizing the golden stream of light passing through you until you have ended your meditation session.

THE OCEAN

Imagine a vast ocean. The ocean is filled with hundreds and thousands of waves. Feel that you are part of that ocean. Imagine that each wave in the ocean is slowly moving through you. Feel that each wave is a wave of joy.

Imagine wave after wave of joy passing through your whole body. As each wave passes through your body, feel that all worries, tensions, anxieties, and problems are being washed away in the successive waves of joy. For several minutes, meditate on wave after wave of joy passing through you. Feel that each new wave of joy that passes through you increases the amount of joy that you now have, until you feel that you have become all joy. Nothing exists for you except limitless, boundless joy.

Now imagine that you are going beneath the surface of the ocean. The surface of the ocean is filled with many waves, but below the surface, in the depths, all is calm, silent, and serene. Imagine yourself sinking slowly into the depths of the ocean. Here there is only calmness, emptiness, and tranquility. As you visualize yourself going deeper and deeper into the depths of the ocean, feel that a profound peace is entering into you. Feel that the deeper you go into the inner ocean, the more peaceful and calm you become.

Visualize that there is no end to the depths of this ocean. It goes on endlessly. Imagine yourself sinking deeper and deeper into this endless ocean of light, feeling more peace and tranquility filling your entire being until you have become all peace and all tranquility. Continue practicing this visualization until you have ended your meditation session.

The Sphere of Power

Practice this technique whenever you feel tension entering into you from outside. This exercise can be practiced while seated, or as part of mindfulness, while you work, talk with others, or engage in any activity. This exercise is particularly effective when you need to stop tension, frustration, or panic immediately.

Focus your attention on the center of your stomach, in the area of your navel. Feel that this is an area of tremendous strength. Visualize a sphere, a dome of red energy surrounding your entire body, which is supported by your own willpower. Positive thoughts, feelings, ideas, and vibrations can pass through this sphere and reach you. But as long as you visualize this sphere of red energy surrounding you, negative thoughts, hostilities, anger, and aggressive feelings of other persons and situations cannot enter you.

While you are visualizing this sphere of red energy surrounding you, feel that you are consciously directing energy from the center of your body, in the area of your navel, throughout the sphere. Feel that the energy of your willpower can easily deflect tension-causing feelings and frustrations that are directed toward you from the outside world. You will find that with repeated practice it becomes easier and easier to visualize this sphere of red energy and that you will be able to stop the negative energy of others from entering you.

THE ROSE

Visualize a beautiful rose in the center of your chest. It is not necessary, when doing this exercise, to see a clear picture of the rose. Simply do the best you can to imagine a soft, reddish rose in the center of your chest. If other thoughts and images pass through your mind while you are performing this exercise, simply ignore them.

Imagine that the rose is completely folded up; none of its petals have yet unfolded. Now, as you focus your attention on the reddish rose in the center of your chest, visualize that the first set of petals, the outer row of petals, is gradually unfolding. As they do so, imagine them growing and expanding and filling the entire area of your chest. Simultaneously feel that a wave of peace and joy is spreading throughout your entire chest area.

Then visualize that a second set of rose petals is unfolding. Imagine them slowly and gently unfolding and expanding, this time filling the entire area of your body. Imagine another wave of peace and joy, even deeper than the first, starting in the center of the chest, in the center of the rose, and expanding outward, filling your entire body with peace and joy. Now visualize a third set of petals, again starting in the center of the rose, and imagine them expanding outward, filling up the entire room, spreading peace and joy everywhere throughout the room or area in which you are meditating.

Then visualize a fourth set of petals opening up, this time expanding and filling the entire earth. Feel that peace and joy are spreading from the center of your chest, from the center of the rose, throughout all of the earth and filling all of the people and all of the beings and all of the objects on this earth with peace and joy.

Now visualize another set of petals opening up, this time filling the entire solar system with peace and bliss. Simultaneously feel that you are spreading your own inner peace, of which you have an infinite supply, throughout the entire solar system.

Finally visualize that a sixth row of petals is opening up, this time filling up the entire universe, spreading peace and joy throughout the universe and on into the infinite.

As you practice this exercise, continue to visualize additional petals of the rose unfolding. As each set of petals unfolds and spreads out into the infinite, feel that they are reaching farther and farther out and spreading a deeper peace and joy throughout your whole being and throughout all of existence. There is no end to the petals of the inner rose. Continue to unfold set after set of petals until you have completed your meditation session.

SWIRLING LIGHT

Focus your attention on the center of your forehead. Visualize that there is a slow but steady swirl of white light there. This particular white light is very soft and gentle. Visualize that the white light above your forehead is slowly moving in a clockwise direction.

Then visualize that the swirling white light is slowly expanding. As it does, the white light begins to encompass the other portions of your body. Imagine the soft white light expanding in a circular swirling motion until your entire body has become lost in it.

Feel that the room you are meditating in is becoming filled with swirling white light. Visualize that the light is expanding beyond the room you are in to encompass the building or area in which you are located. Then imagine that the white light is expanding even farther, encompassing all of the area for miles around you. Finally, visualize the soft white light continuing to expand as it gently swirls around, until it has filled the earth, the sky, the universe, and all of infinity.

Let go. Allow yourself to merge with the slowly swirling calm, peaceful white light. In this timeless light, there is no yesterday, no tomorrow, there is no future or past. Your mind is calm and relaxed. All that exists is swirling white light, and you have become part of that light. Meditate and continue to visualize the swirling white light, experiencing peace and inner stillness, until your meditation session has ended.

PRACTICE TIPS

All of the previously described techniques can be practiced with your eyes open or closed. Most people find that it is easier initially to practice meditation with their eyes closed.

When your mind drifts away from one of the secret meditation techniques, do not become upset or frustrated. Gently move your mind back to the technique you are practicing and begin again. Initially your mind will drift frequently to other subjects, but with practice you will find that your mind's strength quickly grows.

Think of your mind as a muscle. The more you use it, the stronger it will become. However, if you neglect to develop your mind through proper concentration and meditation exercises, it will atrophy and become weaker.

At the end of each meditation session, bow your head toward the ground. Give away your meditation to the universe. Whether you feel you have done well or poorly, simply give your efforts to the universe. Also remember, if you are properly using the secret meditation techniques, you cannot have a "bad" meditation. The only bad meditation is when you don't meditate at all.

Use the previous techniques in rotation. It will prevent your meditation experience from becoming stale, and the different techniques will place you in touch with different fields of auric empowerment, creating a balanced development of your practice.

YANTRA MEDITATION

Yantras are traditional visual aids that are used both externally and internally in the practice of Tantric Buddhism. Yantras are geometrical designs that enable you to focus on an image that will help you to quiet your mind. When you become more advanced in your practice, you will be able to fully visualize a yantra with your eyes closed. Any of the standard yantras in the Tantric texts are suitable for practice.

MANTRA YOGA

Another popular form of meditation is to repeat a mantra and focus on its sound, or its sound in conjunction with a visual image, while practicing meditation. Your root guru will provide you with a personal mantra for you to use. If you do not have access to a root guru, then the best general mantra for practice is: *OM mani padme hum.*

Repeat this mantra, or your personal mantra, for the full period of your meditation session. Do not merely "parrot" a mantra when you are repeating it. Focus your full attention on the mantra you are using until all other thoughts are excluded from your mind.

SOME FINAL CONSIDERATIONS

It is perfectly acceptable to vary your practice. If you wish to use one of the secret techniques for one session, focus on a yantra for another session, and/or focus on a mantra for your next session, this is perfectly acceptable. What is of greatest importance is keeping your mind focused during your periods of meditation and not letting your mind drift. It is far better to do a shorter meditation session with full concentration than a longer session with little or no concentration.

When, during a session, you enter into a period of no-thought, you can stop practicing your visualization, repeating your mantra, or focusing on your yantra. Allow the emptiness, peace, and ecstasy of the thoughtless realm to overwhelm you. When you find yourself starting to think again, refocus on your visualization, yantra, or mantra. Keep practicing in spite of all adverse conditions, and great success will be yours. May all sentient beings attain enlightenment!

The chapter ended here, and I placed *The Handbook* down on the bed. My gaze drifted over to Nadia.

She also had placed her book down and was lying on her back, staring at the ceiling. "What are you reading, Nadia?" I asked her.

"A book on chaos mathematics," she answered, turning her head slightly to the right, looking into my eyes.

"What is that all about?"

"You see, I am studying mathematics, at the university, in Denmark. It's through math that I became interested in Buddhism."

"What is the relationship between Buddhism and math? I don't get it. I thought Buddhism was about enlightenment."

"It is, and so is higher mathematics. Einstein was very interested in enlightenment. He was seeking a unified field theory through which he could explain the interrelationships between time and space, and matter and antimatter."

"So how did chaos math specifically get you interested in Buddhism?" I asked, turning on my left side to face her.

"Well, chaos math is about patterns. The idea is not so complicated. Everyone views life in patterns. When we don't see that something has a pattern, we say it is chaotic. Chaos math is the study of the patterns of chaos. There are countless patterns within what most people would call chaos; in other words, chaos is not really chaotic. It is made up of many different patterns that are not immediately discernable.

"I was once talking to my math teacher, and he told me about the Tantric Buddhist texts. He said that he found something very similar written hundreds of years ago by Buddhist monks in Tibet, which addressed different patterns that they had discovered in the universe that at first glance appeared to be chaotic.

"He had me assist him in creating a computer model of the Buddhist studies to see if they were accurate, and they were. Since my main interest in life is advanced mathematics, I decided to look further into Buddhism to see what else the monks had discovered.

"The more I read, the more I became attracted to the Buddhist philosophy. In the more advanced Buddhist texts I read, they were really talking about concepts that are currently being debated in quantum mechanics. But these Tantric Buddhist texts are centuries old!

"I took a hatha yoga course, that's the physical yoga, at a yoga studio near my school. I enjoyed it very much; it was very relaxing. Then I took a more advanced course that they offered in meditation.

"I started practicing meditation and then read all of the Buddhist books I could get my hands on. I had the opportunity to meet several monks who were visiting Denmark at the time, and they answered many of my questions. But they told me that I had to travel to the East and meet masters who were more advanced than they were if I was really interested in doing more research on the older Tantric texts.

"That's when I suddenly became interested in enlightenment— I mean, it all makes sense to me mathematically."

I smiled at Nadia, and she smiled back. I was somewhat clueless about what she was talking about, but there was one thing I was sure of: I definitely wanted to have sex with her again.

"What are you reading?" she asked in a seductive voice.

"This crazy Oracle, a monk friend of Master Fwap's, gave it to me. It's *The Handbook for Enlightenment*. I guess it's pretty basic compared to the stuff you've read. I don't know yet if I believe in it or not."

Noiselessly, Nadia got up from her cot and came over to my bed and lay down beside me. She sat up for a moment and slowly undid her hair and let it down. She climbed on top of me, and before I knew it, she had lowered her mouth to mine. As we kissed I put my arms around her back and pulled her tightly to my chest.

She then sat up, leaned back on her lovely lower legs, and pulled her sweater off. She told me that she wanted me. She wasn't wearing a bra. With her taut breasts rising above me, and an avalanche of her blond hair spilling down across her shoulders, she began methodically to rub my chest.

"Let's get your shirt off, and this will be easier for both of us," she whispered. I sat up and took off my shirt, then lay down on my back again.

"You must understand that this is not ordinary sex. This is Tantric sex," she murmured, as her hand moved down my chest and began to unbuckle my belt.

"What is Tantric sex, Nadia?" I asked.

"Well, it is a type of yoga. It is one of the many ways to enlightenment. When most people have sex they experience pleasure and perhaps they make a baby, but whether they make a baby or not, they lose energy. That is why most people always fall asleep after they have sex. The point of yoga is to gain energy. When you have enough energy, and you direct it toward enlightened dimensions, you enter into them and they gradually purify your karma, and you become enlightened.

"This can be done," she continued as she unzipped my jeans, "through sex, or just through meditation, or through both. What you must try to grasp is that Tantric sex is meditation. When you meditate while you are having sex, both you and your partner gain energy and enter into higher states of consciousness together. You cannot simply have sex because it feels physically good and claim that it is Tantric sex. Sex should feel good, but in Tantric sex it is important to keep your mind focused on the transmission of the energy between you and your partner."

"Nadia, when we made love last night, I felt a tingly energy flowing back and forth between us. It was different from anything I have ever experienced when I have had sex with any other woman. I saw your aura, too. There were also moments when I found that if I concentrated on the energy that I felt inside of you," I continued, "it would get stronger. Is that what you are talking about?"

"Something like that," she replied in a husky voice. Nadia got up off the bed and removed the rest of her clothes. Then she pulled my pants off and sat down next to me. She was beautiful. As the dim lights of the hostel splashed across her naked body, I wanted her more than anything in the world.

"It is a little more complicated than that," she added.

"How's that?"

"When we make love it is special. We both have more energy than most people, because we meditate. Also, I feel in my heart that we have known each other in past lives—that is why we feel so comfortable together. Tantric sex is something we have experienced together before, in previous incarnations. I intuitively know that this is true.

"The important thing," she remarked as she casually began to stroke my legs, "is to consciously separate our minds from our bodies while we are having sex and join simultaneously in other dimensions. Focus on the energy that is flowing back and forth between us with your whole mind, doing whatever it takes to make it stronger. Then that energy will lift us into higher dimensions of light."

Her hands slowly moved up from my lower legs to my thighs. "I am doing what you are doing. I feel the energy that is in your body and focus on it, and I do anything that I can do with my mind and body to increase the flow of your Kundalini energy, so that we can both go higher.

"Then we'll join in other dimensions. You will see; we will experience each other in new ways in each dimension we come together in."

"Nadia, how do you know all of this?"

"I have read many books about both sexual and nonsexual Tantric yoga. People must meditate and have energy to begin with, and be able to concentrate strongly with their minds, or it will only be ordinary sex. They will lose and not gain energy, and they will become sleepy."

"Nadia, why do I feel so much emotion for you? I hardly know you, and yet I feel like I have always known you."

"Of course you do. We have been together in many, many lifetimes. There is a strong love between us, and it causes us to come back together in each lifetime for a while. That is one of the ways reincarnation works: Whatever you love, you are drawn back to. That is your karma."

She stopped talking and put her mouth down over my already erect penis. She started to move her tongue in a circular motion, while gently sucking. I had experienced oral sex before, but never like this.

As she moved her mouth up and down my penis, she pushed

my thighs up and slightly apart. She started rubbing her palms in a circular motion on the insides of both of my thighs. As soon as she did this, I felt what I can only describe as a bolt of energy shoot from me into her. It was like a lightning flash. This happened repeatedly for several minutes, while she continued to rub my thighs.

I suddenly entered into another dimension, in which I was cascading through a world of light. At the same time, though, another part of me was simultaneously aware of what was happening physically, as my body interacted with Nadia's.

I could feel Nadia's presence in the dimension of light I had entered into, but she was very different there. She seemed to be much stronger in this dimension. I could really feel her power, and somehow I just "knew" that she wanted to join her energy with mine. So I just let go and let it happen. I could feel our life forces striving to combine, and then, in a flash, they merged and became "one."

Physically the oral sex felt ecstatic, but it was nothing compared to the energy rush that was occurring between our nonphysical bodies. I could actually feel telepathically, from Nadia's point of view, what she was experiencing, while at the same time I was aware of my own physical and mental sensations and perceptions. Experiencing both my own sexual ecstasy and hers was almost overwhelming.

I was about to have an orgasm when she pulled her mouth back. "Not yet," she murmured. "The Kundalini energy will get stronger if we wait a little longer. Now it is your turn. Get on top of me."

She rolled onto her left side, and I sat up. Then she lay down on her back and closed her eyes. She slightly parted her legs.

I gently lay on top of her. I was very sexually excited, and I knew that if I entered her at that moment, I would immediately have an orgasm. So I started to kiss her mouth and embrace her instead, in order to give my body a chance to slow down.

Her nipples were very hard against my chest. I began to suck her right breast, then her left breast. As I did, I could feel her life force flowing into me, pushing me into yet another dimension.

As I entered into this new dimension, I suddenly found myself in a world that was composed of golden and blue light. It was also filled with some kind of sparkling greenish dots. Then I saw Nadia's body, but it looked different from her physical body—it was made up of blue light.

We were now in the void together. There was no thought, only a timeless understanding of what existed between us, emotions that there are no words for.

I moved toward her body with my hands outstretched. I noticed that golden light emanated from my palms.

We embraced, and it felt exactly like it had in my dream, when the two of us had been sitting next to each other by the river. There was a sense that we always existed together here in this dimension of beauty and stillness, and that we always would, forever.

Then as suddenly as it had appeared, the dimension of golden and blue light went away, and I found myself back on top of Nadia. My sexual energy had become more even, so I slowly entered her. As I did, she moaned softly.

After moving in and out of her for a few minutes, we changed positions. We sat up, wrapped our legs around each other, and I gently reentered her. Wrapping our arms firmly around each other, we gently rocked back and forth. As she opened her legs a little wider, I thrust more deeply into her. We kissed, and then everything went white.

I don't remember much of what happened after that, except for the two of us passing through countless cascading dimensions of color and ecstasy. In each dimension, our minds would meld in new ways, and something deep and beautiful would pass between us. It was pure telepathy. We were in each other's minds, sharing each other's most intimate thoughts and feelings.

Then Nadia had an orgasm. Her body jerked several times. A few minutes later she had another series of orgasms. Then I came.

Small tears gently started to flow down her face, like mist in the early morning Himalayan sunlight. We embraced for a long time. We eventually separated and curled up together under the rough gray woolen hostel blankets and fell asleep in each other's arms.

I had a dream. In it, Nadia explained to me that she had to go away and find her master, but that we would meet again. She told me that we would always be together in the dimensions of light, even though we would be separated physically. She told me that I should do whatever Master Fwap and the Oracle told me to do. She said that both of them were enlightened.

The dream then shifted. I was snowboarding down a large mountain, carving wide edges in new powder, when I heard a rumbling sound behind me. I quickly glanced over my shoulder and saw that an avalanche had started and was about to come crashing down on me.

I snowboarded straight to pick up speed, but it didn't help. Snow was everywhere, and suddenly I was buried under it. The world went white for a minute, and then black. The last thing I remember thinking was that I felt very cold.

When I woke up, I reached over for Nadia, but she had left. I looked over at her bunk, and in the early morning Katmandu light that was filtering down through the hostel's small upper dormitory windows, I could see that her bunk was empty and that her backpack was gone.

She had left me while I was dreaming. I had lost her somewhere in a virtual avalanche of endless snow.

8

The Kundalini Poster Girl

After lying in bed for a while contemplating Nadia's disappearance, I finally got up, showered, shaved, dressed, and headed out onto the streets of Katmandu. I decided to look for her, although my second attention was already telling me that I wasn't going to find her.

But still, my mind insisted that I search for her, so I started a systematic pattern sweep of all of the shops in town where the college crowd tended to hang. No luck. After about four hours of roaming the streets, poking my head in and out of shops and stores, I gave up.

I was definitely depressed. I mean, I had finally met my soul mate, or whatever, and after having perfect sex and falling in love with her, she had split. Major bummer.

Then the weirdest thing began happening to me. I suppose it was just subconscious machinations in visual form, but I began to see her face on all of the posters in town.

Most of the shops and coffee bars in Katmandu plaster their walls with posters, the majority of them being of Indian and American film stars. Each time I glanced at a female actress's poster, I saw Nadia's face. Her clear blue eyes would be staring at me through the eyes of the different female stars on the posters, and I could feel her talking telepathically to me through them.

I got the drift already, it was over. She had her enlightened thing to do, and she had to follow her karma. She was gone. I could respect that. I suppose I would have continued looking for her, but enlightenment was just not high on my priority list at the time, snowboarding was. So for the second time in my life, my passion for snowboarding took me away from the second perfect woman in my life.

I was totally bummed. I was also pissed off at Master Fwap and the Oracle. I mean, what was the point of setting me up with the perfect woman, only to have her split on me? I thought Buddhism was supposed to help you get away from your pain, not increase it.

I drifted back to the hostel. A new crew of mountaineers, hippies, and enlightenment-seeking types had just checked in. Everyone else I had known there was gone. The hostel had heavy turnover.

Some of the new women were pretty and obviously on the prowl for more than just enlightenment, but after what I had experienced for the last two days with Nadia, I just wasn't interested.

Lying down on my bunk, I covered my face with my pillow and tried to get some sleep, but it didn't work. I just lay there thinking about Nadia.

When I'm overtired, my mind plays funny tricks on me. Lying on my bunk, with a pillow over my head, feeling very sorry for myself, I started to see Nadia in my mind's eye. She was dressed in a stunning evening gown, as some of the female actresses had been dressed in the posters I had seen that day. Her eyes radiated warmth and compassion. In a very odd way, they reminded me of

Master Fwap's eyes. Then it came to me: Nadia was the Kundalini poster girl.

I imagined posters of her all over the world, advertising meditation and enlightenment. The absurdity of my idea made me laugh and I began to wonder how I had managed to get so attached to a woman in just two days.

My Himalayan trip was suddenly not going as I had planned. Instead of being out on the greatest slopes in the world, carving in and out of perfect powder, I felt I was first being pulled into some weird Buddhist Order by Master Fwap, and now I was lying around feeling depressed over some woman I hardly knew.

I had to change things around. I would put Master Fwap, the Oracle, Nadia, and all of this enlightenment nonsense behind me and return to my snowboarding. The next day I would hit the slopes and reboot my trip. With these thoughts in my mind, I was finally able to get some much-needed sleep.

9

Extreme Vertical "R" Us

The next day totally sucked. I arose before dawn and didn't even meditate. Instead I headed for the mountains, deciding I would clear my head of Nadia, Master Fwap and the Oracle. I set out to snowboard the most extreme vertical slope I had ever attempted.

I hitched a ride right away and within a couple of hours reached the highest point that the road led to. From here it was climbing time. I got my gear out of the truck, thanked the driver, and started to ascend the peak.

I just knew for some reason that this was going to be a one-run day. I figured it would take me about four hours of hiking just to get to the top of the peak, allowing me time for only one ultimately gnarly, vertical run. Halfway through my climb it started to snow, the temperature dropped, and I could hardly see where I was going.

"Fuck it!" I thought to myself. I was definitely pissed off at myself, the world, the weather, the mountains, and everything and everyone else in the universe. If I had been thinking more clearly, I would have started to descend the mountain and head back to Katmandu. This would have been a challenging run even in ideal conditions, but with lousy visibility and frigid temperatures, it was now both dangerous and stupid to even attempt.

I have never been afraid of dying. Naturally, my body has felt fear many times, but the thought of death has never bothered me. Maybe that is why I continued up the mountain that day, or maybe I was just trying to punish myself.

It took two hours longer than I had figured to reach the top of the peak. The sun was already beginning to set. Between the snow and the diminishing light I could barely see anything. I knew I was doing something stupid, but at this point there was nothing I could do about it.

I was freezing cold, exhausted by the climb, gasping for breath because of the thinness of the air, and pissed off and depressed at my current situation in life. This was definitely not the best state of mind to be in for the most challenging vertical run I had ever attempted.

I unstrapped my snowboard from my back, changed from my climbing to snowboarding boots, shouldered my day pack, and put on my goggles. I thought that I would probably die in the next few minutes on the first section of the vertical drop, end up in a snowy grave, and that would be that.

With nothing to lose, I snapped my snowboarding boots into their bindings on my jet-black snowboard, and I started down the mountain.

I was snow-blind. At best, I could see about ten feet ahead of myself at any given time. I just let my reflexes take over, and I started to descend fast.

I did better than I thought I would. I managed to do a series of sharp razor cuts and survived the most extreme vertical section of the mountain. The slope then started to even out a little, but the wind suddenly kicked up, blowing the rapidly falling snow into huge white swirling clouds all around me. The visibility dropped to about four feet ahead of my board. Conditions were not good.

Somehow I managed to keep descending, and after a while it began to occur to me that I might make it down the mountain in one piece after all. The snow stopped and the clouds parted. I could see the bright descending sun against a pure blue Nepalese sky.

Then I saw the crevasse. It was about twenty feet across, and to compound the problem, on the other side of the crevasse there was another sharp vertical slope that went straight up.

I had no other choice but to try and jump the crevasse. Even if I managed to clear the crevasse, I was going to smack straight into the vertical slope on the other side.

I started the jump, and I'm sure it would have made a great photograph, at least the before shot. There I was, dressed in my rad red parka and boarding pants, doing a perfect transboarding jump between two opposing slopes, with the descending sun hanging in the blue Nepalese sky behind me. . . . It was definitely a Kodak moment—my last.

I hit the opposing slope hard and almost fell over before I fishtailed and started to board backward. I quickly threw all of my weight to my right, to avoid getting sucked down into the crevasse, did a one-eighty flip, and was then headed straight down the mountain again. I don't know how I pulled it off, but somehow I was still standing on my board carving my way down the mountain!

The slope became more gradual and I slowed my pace, taking my time descending, making wide curves in the snow. When I reached the bottom of the slope, it was almost totally dark. I got off my board, sat down on it, and realized that I was probably both the luckiest and dumbest snowboarder on earth.

After changing my boots and shouldering my board and day pack, I walked down to the rock and gravel road that led back to Katmandu. I walked in the darkness for about half an hour before I hitched a ride with a couple of Indian tourists in a Toyota Land Cruiser. They dropped me off at the hostel. After climbing the stairs to the dorm and finding my bunk, I removed my gear, lay down, and immediately fell asleep. I was so tired that it never even occurred to me to eat.

10

THE SANTA MONICA BLUES

When I woke up the next morning, I decided it was time to return to California. I was sensible enough to know that my snowboarding was getting out of control and that I needed a change of scene. I decided to go back to see some friends in Santa Monica, figuring I would do some surfing and return to my old life.

In the back of my mind, I harbored the thought that one day I might return to the Himalayas, but I seriously doubted it. While I loved both Master Fwap and Nadia, they just weren't like me. My world was competitive athletics, and theirs was enlightenment. It just seemed to me "never the twain shall meet."

I gathered up all my belongings, what little there were, and made travel arrangements back to the United States. I was more than happy to be getting out of Katmandu.

I flew back the next day. After landing at Los Angeles International Airport, I cleared Customs and grabbed a cab to Santa Monica.

It was late afternoon in L.A., and the freeways were full of cars, the whole landscape one big smogged-out parking lot. The cab driver wisely decided to avoid the freeways, staying on the surface streets instead. We reached Santa Monica in about forty minutes.

I shared a condo on Santa Monica Boulevard with three other surfers. When I arrived no one was at home, so I assumed they were all out catching the late-afternoon swells.

I was exhausted and was feeling a little weird about being back in the fast-paced world of California with its rock music, freeway nightmares, and "party on, dude" mentality. Although I was having trouble consciously admitting it, even though I'd been back for less than an hour, I already missed the Himalayas.

Like most people who live in or around L.A., I have a love-hate relationship with the city. The beaches are beautiful, the people are easygoing, the surfing is good, and the snowboarding in the local mountains is adequate. Its other two outstanding features, from my point of view, are that it is home to thousands of the most beautiful women in the world, and world-class snowboarding is just a short plane ride away in Colorado and Utah.

A great many of the most beautiful women in America come to L.A. assuming that they will instantly become mega-movie or TV goddesses if they just get discovered. The vast majority of them, however, end up with short-lived walk-on parts in soaps and spend most of their time waiting tables and standing in long audition lines.

The good news is for the L.A. guy. If you're rich, famous, a producer, or a director, you can definitely get laid every night by a different beautiful woman if you want to. This situation is also good for studly young surfer types. For some reason, there is a heavy physical attraction thing between aspiring wanna-be actress types and surfer dudes.

My problem with L.A. was that I could see the air I was breathing, I don't particularly like crowds, and I was much better at snowboarding than I was at surfing. Since L.A. is definitely a party scene, its attraction for me was ephemeral.

Okay, so why did I live in L.A. in the first place? I had been asking myself that for a while. I liked the warm weather and I liked my roommates, Bob, Jeff, and Sandy. They were all excellent surfers. I had tried to get them into snowboarding, but to no avail. I would go surfing with them up at Zuma Beach when I was in town, and we definitely enjoyed one another's company.

I walked around the condo for a while, familiarizing myself with it, reached for the phone, then hung it up again. Who was I going to call? I wandered around like this for a while.

I was too tired to fall asleep, so I got my surfboard and wet suit out of the closet, hopped into my '67 beige V.W. bug, and headed up the Pacific Coast Highway to Malibu.

The traffic wasn't too bad, and I made it up to Zuma Beach in about forty-five minutes. As I pulled into the parking lot, I got a look at the waves, which were much bigger than I had expected.

I parked and locked my car, changed into my Body Glove suit, and headed for the swells. Paddling out to my spot, lo and behold—Bob, Jeff, and Sandy were all occupying our usual salty turf.

Sandy spotted me first. He gave me a quick nod as he caught a left-breaking wave. I paddled over to Bob and Jeff and greeted them.

"What's with the big waves?" I asked. "Is there a storm coming in or something?"

"No, man," Bob said, smiling, "it's 'Big Wednesday.' "

"Big Wednesday" is an intrinsic part of the surfer mythology. According to surf legends, the biggest waves always happen on Wednesdays. I had never seen any discernible difference between the waves on Wednesdays as opposed to other days, but for whatever reason, today was definitely "Big Wednesday."

Both Bob and Jeff caught the next wave together. It was a long curl that broke fast on the inside. I decided to hang in the water for a while until something a little smaller came along. After a few minutes I saw the wave I wanted, started paddling with my hands, and then stood up on my board and caught it. It was a super clean ride in. After my last snowboarding experience in the Himalayas, it definitely felt good to be back in the water.

We surfed until sunset and then hit the beach. There were a bunch of other surfers hanging around, waiting for the "Blue Flash," so we joined them. On clear days, there is a moment, just after the sun dips behind the ocean, when a flash of blue light shoots across the water. I had seen it a few times but never as strongly as that day.

"'Big Wednesday,' man," Sandy said with a sigh. "Well, let's pack it up and party on!"

Everybody loaded their gear into their cars and drove down the Pacific Coast Highway back to our condo in Santa Monica. We all showered and then dressed in our blue jeans and surfer shirts. Now the question was, what was on for the night?

"It's good to see you back, man," Bob remarked. "Like, it's been quiet without you. How was the boarding over there?"

"Most excellent!" I said, putting on my best L.A. smile, which obviously wasn't fooling anyone.

"Come on, my man, what you need is to party out," Sandy yelled with enthusiasm. "We have some serious action set up for tonight. There's a wild sorority party over at U.C.L.A. that we've been invited to. It's going to be a long night, man. Long and good."

The U.C.L.A. campus is located in Westwood, about twenty-five minutes from Santa Monica. All of the major fraternity houses are adjacent to the west side of the campus, and the sorority houses border it on the east.

When we arrived, it was a madhouse. Music was blaring, tequila, vodka, and beer were flowing, and couples were all over each other on couches, the floor, and—I assumed—upstairs in the bedrooms.

We went over to the bar and Sandy immediately took charge. He ordered us all shots of tequila, with lite beer chasers. After we had belted down about six shots each, Bob and Jeff drifted off and started dancing with some attractive co-eds, leaving me alone at the bar with Sandy.

"What's up, man? Is something the matter?" Sandy asked me, his voice now slightly slurred from the tequila, as he sat down on the bar stool next to me. "You don't seem to be getting into the spirit of the party."

"It's probably just jet lag, Sandy. I'm sure I'll feel better in a little while."

"Well, my man, let me help you out. Let me speed the process. There's nothing that will put you into a better space faster than a fine lady. There is someone here I want you to meet. She just broke up with her boyfriend, and now she's on the rebound. I think you two will hit it off."

"It's cool, Sandy. I just need some space, that's all. The Himalayan thing just left me in a strange place. It's going to take a few more days to adjust to being back in the Western world, that's all."

"No way, dude. You can't cop out on this. You definitely have to connect with Carol. She's a sociology major, and that's what you need right now, some righteous socialization! Let me go hunt her up. Now don't go away, I'll be right back."

Before I could object, Sandy had backed away from the bar and disappeared into the crowd. As I sat at the bar drinking myself into oblivion, I felt more and more that I just wanted to be alone. Something was nagging at my subconscious, but for the life of me I couldn't figure out what it was.

I asked the bartender for another shot, downed it, and just as I was about to order another, Sandy appeared with a very attractive woman on his arm.

He introduced us and then walked away, looking, I assumed, for someone to pick up. I was left sitting alone at the bar with Carol. I decided to make polite conversation.

"Sandy tells me you're a sociology major. What made you pick sociology?"

"Well," she replied in a relaxed L.A. Valley Girl tone of voice, "when I graduate, I want to work with kids who come from troubled backgrounds, although I may decide to get my master's degree first. What do you do?"

I looked at Carol for a moment, conjuring up an answer. I was pretty drunk, and she looked, what shall we say, very appealing. She was about five foot two, had brunette hair, was slim, and had beautiful jade green eyes. She was wearing a short black cocktail dress, which did not leave a great deal to the imagination.

"I'm mainly into sports. I surf, snowboard, do martial arts, and mountain climb. I'm not in school right now. I thought I would take some time off and travel. As a matter of fact, I just got back from Nepal today."

"Where do you live?"

"In Santa Monica, on the Boulevard. I share a condo there with Sandy and two other dudes. We all surf together."

"I see," she said, pausing to assess me.

"How about a drink? What would you like?"

"Vodka and tonic with a twist, please."

I ordered her drink and another shot for myself. After we had finished our drinks, I asked Carol if she wanted to dance. She agreed, and the two of us headed for the dance floor.

On the floor, couples were gyrating back and forth to some heavy rap. We began to dance, and in a few minutes I started to feel better. Dancing is always an instant "up" for me, and Carol was a better than average dancer. Pretty soon we started to smile at each other, and the sexual energy started flowing between us.

We danced for about an hour. Then we hit the bar for a few more drinks.

"Would you like to come up and see my room? It's just up the stairs."

"Sure."

I had been drinking a lot, and judging from the shaky way Carol ascended the stairs, she was pretty high too. Carol led me into her all-pink sorority room and closed the door. The two of us fell down on the bed and started making out. A few minutes later our clothes had been shed and we were having sex. I remember Carol laughing a lot and talking after we had finished making love. Then everything got hazy and I passed out.

When I awoke some time during the night, the party had ended, and I was alone in a bedroom with Carol, on the second floor of her sorority house. I was still drunk and starting to get seriously depressed.

Carol was lying next to me asleep. I liked Carol. The sex had been fun. During the course of the evening she had told me all about her two brothers, Ron and Michael, who worked as producers at Capitol Records, about her father, who was working at Hughes Aircraft on the new Stealth Bomber, and about her mother's addiction to sitcoms. I had also learned a great deal more about sociology than I really wanted to know.

Try as I would, I just couldn't fall back asleep. My main problem was that I kept thinking about Nadia. I felt strange lying next to Carol and thinking about another woman, particularly because Carol was so attractive, intelligent, fun, and more on my wavelength than Nadia had been.

Carol wasn't forcing me into the mysterious world of Buddhism, magic, and mysticism. She was a normal, healthy, bright U.C.L.A. co-ed who shared my interest in sex, rock and roll, and dancing. She was an all-American girl with a good sense of self-esteem, sensitivity, and career goals ... and she bored the absolute hell out of me.

Without disturbing Carol, I slipped out of bed, noiselessly put my clothes back on, and exited from the sorority house. I had no idea where my roommates had disappeared to, but I assumed they were all sharing rooms with good-looking co-eds somewhere within the sorority.

I hopped into my V.W., drove up Sorority Row to Sunset Boulevard, and then headed west toward the ocean. According to my watch it was a little after three o'clock in the morning.

Crossing over the 405 Highway on Sunset, I continued driving west through Pacific Palisades until I reached the Pacific Coast Highway. I turned right at Gladstone's 4 Fish, and proceeded to drive up north to Malibu.

I had no idea where I was going or why. I was just driving.

In about thirty minutes I had reached Zuma Beach. I turned left off the highway, but instead of turning into the beach parking lot, I turned onto Heather Cliff Lane instead.

I followed the curving road up to the top of Point Dume. Along the way, the strong smell of the eucalyptus trees that lined the road blew in through my open car windows.

Parking my car near the end of the point, I proceeded on foot to the top of the cliff at the very end of the point. From there I could look out over the moonlit Pacific Ocean that I loved so much. On my left side I could see the glittering lights of Los Angeles, and to my right the dark stretches of Zuma Beach and Broad Beach that were punctuated by house and street lights.

I directed my gaze back out toward the moonlit Pacific. I watched the concentric wave patterns moving toward the bottom of Point Dume, where they crashed loudly on the rocks below me.

For the moment, I had stopped thinking. Standing alone in the night with the ocean wind buffeting my body. I felt as if I was back in the Himalayas. This feeling lasted for several minutes. I then descended the hill, returned to my car, and drove home to Santa Monica. When I got home, I lay down on my bed and was overwhelmed with the greatest feeling of despair and loneliness I had ever known.

II

I DREAM OF MASTER FWAP

Snow was falling all around me as I walked alone down a Himalayan mountain road, through a sunless valley. I saw a figure in the distance approaching me. As the figure got closer, I recognized that it was Master Fwap. When we reached each other, the two of us stopped and stared at each other.

"Are you ready to come back to the Himalayas and resume your quest for the secret of the missing dimensions with the Oracle and me? You still haven't solved the riddle yet, or have you forgotten about that?"

I didn't know what to say, so I remained silent.

"Come back to Nepal. Los Angeles has provided you with what you would call a 'reality check,' has it not?"

I still said nothing.

"It is necessary to compare and contrast things, in order to know if they are true or not. Buddha said that we shouldn't believe any of his teachings until we have personally validated them through our own experiences. Now that you have returned to your old life in Los Angeles, it gives you the perspective you need to see if your experiences in the Himalayas were worthwhile."

I still remained silent.

"You cannot lie to yourself. You know that you were much happier in Nepal than you have been since your return."

"Yes, but Master Fwap, all of this enlightenment, meditation, Tantric sex, past life memories, karma, and all the rest of it, I mean, why me? I'm just a jock. Nadia wants enlightenment, you and the Oracle say I am destined to become enlightened, but I still don't even know what it is that I want," I said in an unhappy tone of voice.

"You worry too much. In Christianity, what you are now experiencing is referred to as the 'dark night of the soul.' None of us really choose our own destinies; it is simply our egos that cause us to think that we do. Our destinies are chosen by a higher power, nirvana. It is only our egos that make us think that we are the doers and the deciders.

"Do whatever makes you feel happy," he continued gently. "If staying in Los Angeles pleases you, then remain there. But if your experiences with Buddhism in the Himalayas made you happier, then return."

"Master Fwap, I was happy with Nadia, but to be honest, you and the Oracle scare the hell out of me. Will I ever see her again?"

"Perhaps you will. Life is not always predictable. If you return to Katmandu now, you will discover that she has left. She has to follow her karma, just as you do. My advice to you, as your spiritual teacher, is to fulfill your karmic destiny by returning to the Himalayas and solving the riddle. Then you can go back to America, or go wherever you like. Do not let your fears deter you from doing what is right. Also, if I am not mistaken, there are still many mountains in the Himalayas that you have not yet snowboarded.

"Return to Nepal at once. Come to my monastery, and join me and the Oracle on our journey deep into the Anapurna range.

Come home to Nepal. By the way, the Oracle likes you quite a bit. He told me that no one has made him laugh quite as much as you have for several incarnations!"

The dream changed, and I was alone again on the road, with the snow lightly blowing around me.

The next morning when I awoke, I lay in my bed for a few minutes, listening to the sounds of the busy L.A. traffic outside my window. Los Angeles was alive and on the prowl.

I got up, showered, shaved, and dressed. I had made a big decision. I called my low-budget travel agent and booked a flight for the next day to Katmandu. Master Fwap was right, I could feel it in my gut. Running away had never been the answer for me, nor would it be now. I had to return to the East to finish what I had started.

There was a difference this time. On my first trip to Nepal, my goal had been to surf the Himalayas. While that hadn't changed, I now had a second goal as well—to solve the riddle of the missing dimensions, and to see, as Master Fwap claimed, if it was possible to turn my snowboarding into a form of Buddhist meditation.

If I could do that, then I would not only have succeeded at surfing the Himalayas, but I would also have taken a shot at perhaps the wildest ride in the universe—snowboarding to nirvana.

As I mentally prepared for my return, I silently started to repeat the American snowboarder's mantra, "No guts, no glory," over and over. The snowy ranges of the Himalayas were waiting for me on the roof of the world.

PART TWO

The Secret

of the Missing

Dimensions

12

I THINK OF NOTHING

A couple of days after leaving L.A., I arrived at Master Fwap's monastery. It was early in the morning, and I had brought all of my gear, including my two snowboards, with me. Master Fwap greeted me at the entrance with a beaming smile. Without saying a word, he gestured to me to follow him into his monastery, down a long dark corridor, and into the main meditation room.

I placed my gear on the floor and followed him over to the altar, which was located at the north end of the room. It was covered with small flickering candles, a large Buddha statue, burning incense, and fresh flowers. Above the altar was a large Tibetan *thanka*, which consisted of a picture of Padma Sambava, the founder of Tibetan Tantric Buddhism, that had been painted on cloth in bright reds, greens, aquas, golds, purples, and blacks.

In the painting, Padma Sambava was seated in a meditation pose, holding a *dorje* (the symbol of power in Tibetan Buddhism) in one hand and a lotus flower in his other hand. On the same piece of cloth, above, below, and around him, were paintings of other deities, fluffy clouds, and bowls of fresh fruit.

The intricate cloth painting of Padma Sambava was surrounded by two narrow red-and-yellow pieces of brocade cloth. The entire cloth painting had then been mounted on a second, much larger piece of blue brocade, which was decorated with flowers and what appeared to be spoke-filled wheels. Parts of the brocade were very faded, and I assumed that the *thanka* must be very old.

The Oracle was in front of me, sitting to the right of the altar on a large, ornate meditation cushion. He was dressed as he had been the first day I had met him, in a bright ocher robe with a red sash. Several strings of stone beads tied together by some kind of black cord hung around his neck. His eyes were closed, and I assumed that he was in deep meditation.

Master Fwap indicated with a glance from his eyes that I should take a seat in front of the altar. Sitting on a small, greenish meditation cushion between Master Fwap and the Oracle, I closed my eyes and tried to meditate.

The smell of the Nepalese incense that flooded the room brought back memories of many Sunday mornings I had spent as a child sitting in church. In the midst of my childhood recollections, I began to wonder if I hadn't made an error by returning to Katmandu. For no apparent reason, I suddenly felt uncomfortable and strangely alienated, sitting between these two elderly holy men, having just returned from the totally sensed-out world of Los Angeles.

The three of us sat in this manner in silence for about an hour. I kept mentally reassuring myself that I had done the right thing by returning. I was aware that my consciousness was not exactly frosty after my "dark night of the soul" adventures in Los Angeles, and I couldn't help but wonder if my Santa Monica–ized aura was polluting the sacred vibration of Master Fwap's incense-filled meditation hall.

I then opened my eyes, and as I did, I saw that Master Fwap and the Oracle were simultaneously bowing, touching their foreheads to the cold, stone temple floor. I imitated their movements as best I could, bowing and touching the floor with my forehead just as they had done. I didn't want to offend any of their Buddhist traditions, even though I didn't see much point to bowing and offering my meditation to the universe—as had been recommended in *The Handbook for Enlightenment*—since all I had done for the last hour was think about my doubts instead of slowing and stopping my thoughts and entering into a meditative state.

After bowing, Master Fwap and the Oracle sat up and looked at me. The Oracle was the first to speak: "I am glad you have returned from America. It takes great courage to come to a foreign land in search of truth. Tomorrow we will begin our journey into the depths of the Anapurna range, but today we should converse and relax. Tomorrow we will need all of the strength we can command for the long and harsh road that lies ahead of us.

"It is important at times to talk about enlightenment," the Oracle continued in a serious tone of voice. "Even though it is impossible to accurately express the higher truths of eternity in words, it is still very helpful to discuss them. Engaging in what we refer to as 'Buddhist high talk' helps us to clarify and strengthen our consciousness.

"Your mind must be strong and clear enough to understand and accept the Buddhist reasons for following the pathway to enlightenment. Even though much of what we will talk about today will be beyond your capacity to understand, our conversation will still be of great assistance to the logical side of your mind, whose help you will need in order to pursue the seemingly obscure metaphysical truths of Buddhism.

"Your mind needs 'reasons' for pursuing what appears, from its Western perspective, to be ritualistic forms of Buddhist practice and behavior. You have not had an Eastern cultural education in which you would have been taught from childhood forward the

129

positive gains that engaging in these practices and forms of behavior will bring to your entire life over the course of time."

"The truth is," Master Fwap interjected, "that all of life's phenomena are really empty. From the Buddhist perspective, all of life's pursuits, including the pursuit of enlightenment itself, are illusory."

"Well then," I inquired as I directed my eyes toward Master Fwap, "why would you want me to seek enlightenment if it is really only an illusion? That doesn't make much sense to me."

"Oh, but it does, my young American friend, it does," he said as a gentle smile crossed his aged face. "Please be patient with my traditional Buddhist monk ways. I will explain to you why this is so.

"Enlightenment, as I have told you before, is beyond your mind's understanding. You can experience it, talk about it, and ultimately even know and become 'one' with it, and yet your intellect will never completely understand what enlightenment truly is."

"Pardon me, but, that doesn't exactly make a whole lot of sense either. How can I experience something, be able to discuss it, know it, and 'be' it, but not be able to intellectually understand what it is I am experiencing, discussing, knowing, and becoming? I don't get it. Please help me out here."

"It is easy to talk about enlightenment," he said, rapidly responding to my question. "For example, I can say that enlightenment is perfection, bliss, and ecstasy, or that it provides an end to suffering. I can also explain to you about both the philosophy and cosmology of Buddhism. In addition, I can inform you of the secret practices and the meditation techniques of Tantric Buddhism and explain how to perform them. And if you follow my instructions to the letter, then after many years of practice, you will experience enlightenment personally. You will both know it and have 'become' it. But still you won't intellectually understand what enlightenment is, or what it means to have become it."

I was becoming frustrated. "How can that be possible? To me, what you are saying is completely illogical."

"Well, I don't understand the first thing about enlightenment, even though I am enlightened. Perhaps the Oracle understands it better than I do. Do you, O enlightened Oracle of Nepal?" Master Fwap asked, turning his attention to the Oracle.

Following Master Fwap's glance, I looked over at the Oracle to see if he had anything to say that would help me make sense out of Master Fwap's seemingly contradictory statements. He was silent for a few minutes, and then in a singsong tone of voice he said, "Personally, I have been enlightened for countless incarnations. As a matter of fact, I cannot remember an age in which I was not enlightened. But I am afraid I am in the same position that Fwap is; even though I am enlightened, I really don't understand the first thing about it.

"Enlightenment," he continued, "cannot be understood here, in this three-dimensional world that you call home. You may think that you understand it, but if you do you are only allowing your mind to play a trick on you. Your so-called understanding of enlightenment will at best only be a dry, conceptual understanding, since enlightenment resides in worlds that are beyond conceptual knowledge."

Master Fwap smoothly cut in, "We see this happen here in Nepal all the time. Young people from the Western cultures come to the Himalayas with the idea that enlightenment can be gained through discussions with enlightened masters. These young people, many of whom are very bright, are absolutely convinced that once enlightenment has been explained to them, they will have intellectually grasped the concept of enlightenment and will have therefore attained it!

"So we normally play a little Buddhist joke on them. You see, truly enlightened Tantric Buddhist monks, like the Oracle and myself, have quite a sense of humor.

"We tell these would-be seekers of enlightenment, who have traveled so far from the West, whatever it is that they want to hear. When we see that they have become convinced enough through our conversations with them that they understand what enlightenment is, and in their own minds believe that they have attained it, we assure them that they have gained true 'understanding' of enlightenment, and then we encourage them to return to their homes."

"That doesn't sound very honest to me, Master Fwap and Master Oracle. I thought Buddhist monks weren't suppose to tell lies."

"We're not telling lies," Master Fwap responded with a broad grin. "Are we, O enlightened Oracle of Nepal?"

The Oracle shook his head vigorously from side to side several times before replying. "No, of course not. It's impossible for enlightened Buddhist monks to tell lies."

"You see," Master Fwap went on to explain, the smile on his face quickly enlarging, "we are telling the young Western seekers of enlightenment the truth. In all honesty, through our discussions with them, they have gained a completely accurate intellectual 'understanding' of enlightenment. We absolutely tell them the truth, but we just leave out something; we skip the part about the fact that an intellectual 'understanding' of enlightenment is not the same as knowing, experiencing, and becoming enlightened."

"Now is that fair, Master Fwap? If someone travels all the way from the West to come here and to find out what the higher truths of life are and to become enlightened, and you only explain it to

132

them, but don't further explain that the explanation of enlightenment that you have given him isn't the same as really being enlightened, then . . . if you'll excuse my language . . . that's fucked."

"Not at all," the Oracle said with a hearty laugh. "It's a joke."

"A joke?" I asked in a plaintive and confused voice. "Why would you want to play a joke on someone who is searching for enlightenment and truth?"

"For two reasons," Master Fwap responded with a gentle laugh. "The first reason is simply because it's so funny. Now, at first you may not understand our Buddhist sense of humor, so humor me for a moment, and I will endeavor to explain it to you."

"Okay," I said hesitantly, "but this better make sense."

"Imagine," he began, "someone who travels all the way from the West in search of enlightenment. This, as the Oracle remarked before, takes great courage in and of itself. In order for a young person to leave their 'modern' first world country, with all of its comforts and conveniences, and to join us here in our antiquated, physically impoverished, uneducated, and unsophisticated third world country, they must be highly motivated.

"Naturally, as Buddhist monks, we respect this courage and motivation, but courage and motivation are not enough for the true attainment of enlightenment. In addition to these qualities, an individual—whether from the West or the East—must have what I can only describe as a 'bright curiosity,' an ability to see through our Tantric Buddhist fabrications. We create our Tantric Buddhist fabrications, as our masters and their masters did, to gently eliminate individuals who we see are not yet truly ready for the hardships and demands of the practices that lead to nonconceptual enlightenment."

"What are Tantric Buddhist fabrications?"

"A Tantric Buddhist fabrication," Master Fwap continued in

a patient and dignified tone of voice, "is a test. It is necessary to test a potential student to see if he is strong enough to endure the rigors of the path. It is one thing to learn how to meditate and experience higher states of consciousness, that requires some effort. But to become fully enlightened and realize nirvana, that's truly challenging.

"So if we see that someone we have met and talked with about enlightenment is content with the intellectual explanation we have provided them with, then we know that they are not ready to learn the secret Tantric Buddhist methods and the secret meditation techniques that lead an individual to nonconceptual enlightenment and finally the entrance into *paranirvana*.

"Assured by us that they have fully intellectually grasped enlightenment—which in truth they have, at least on an intellectual level—we then encourage them to return to their homeland. They then do so convinced that they now not only know what enlightenment is, but that they have attained it!

"Some of them even write books about enlightenment, intellectually explaining it to other people in the cultures they have returned to. No doubt their intellectual explanations are correct, but they really have nothing to do with the true experience and 'knowing' of enlightenment at all.

"Lord Buddha was very specific about this very point," Master Fwap continued, emphasizing his words in a stronger tone of voice. "Buddha explained to his disciples that enlightenment cannot be explained. He made it very clear to them through his discourses on the dharma that enlightenment can be attained only through an individual's practice of meditation, and that all of the explanations and rituals that are often associated with self-discovery will not lead a person to true enlightenment.

"Buddha further revealed to his disciples," Master Fwap continued explaining, "that all of the sutras, tantras, and fine discourses that he gave to his disciples about enlightenment were really quite worthless. They were, as he said, 'only hollow words.' "

"If they were only hollow words, why did he bother uttering them at all?"

"A good question," remarked the Oracle.

"Buddha, and every enlightened master before and since him," Master Fwap responded, "has made it abundantly clear to anyone who would actually listen carefully to what he said, that enlightenment can be experienced only through the actual practice of meditation. The more you 'understand' enlightenment, the less you really 'know' it.

"Your intellectual understanding of enlightenment only fools you into thinking that you have attained the genuine article. If that is the case, and you actually believe that you have attained it when in fact you have only a cursory intellectual understanding of enlightenment, then you will be satisfied, and your quest will end right then and there. You will return to your homeland convinced that you have actually become enlightened."

"This phenomenon also happens frequently here in the East," the Oracle added. "The East is filled with Buddhist, Hindu, and Taoist masters who really believe that they have attained enlightenment, because they have gained a deeper 'intellectual' understanding of enlightenment, in comparison with the average person who meditates.

"These masters are not consciously lying. From a Buddhist point of view, when they tell their followers and others that they are enlightened, they are not lying because they truly believe that they have attained enlightenment. And since no enlightened person has bothered to contradict them, what they tell others about their 'attainment' is said in all innocence."

"Enlightenment cannot be known through the reading of books, or listening to lofty discourses," Master Fwap cut in. "You must experience it directly. It is like your snowboarding. I'm sure a person could read all about snowboarding, its methods and techniques, and have an excellent understanding of what it is and how to do it just by reading about it. But that doesn't mean that they could then go and successfully snowboard down a mountain on their first snowboarding outing without proper instruction and practice, does it?"

"No, of course not," I responded.

"Well," Master Fwap continued, "it is the same with enlightenment. We have a lot of explanations and methods, practices and approaches, that we explain through words and concepts, or are depicted graphically in the *thankas* and mandalas, but their purpose is not to transmit enlightenment. Their purpose is to inspire the student first to learn and then to go and practice meditation until they have directly experienced enlightenment itself, in all of its radiant glory."

"Oh, I get it. It's like reading about how great it feels to ride high when you're snowboarding. It turns you on to the sport or inspires you, and then you go and give it a try."

"That's correct," Master Fwap responded with a smile. "So perhaps now you can understand why we weave our Tantric Buddhist tapestry of illusions for prospective students of enlightenment. If they seem fully content with our intellectual explanations, which is more often the case than not, then we let them go. This is our way of weeding out the students of enlightenment who will not succeed. It is like one of your precollege examinations that eliminate prospective students who would not succeed in college.

"It is only a rare seeker of truth who will insist on more than our intellectual explanations of enlightenment. They will see through the hollowness of our Tantric Buddhist tapestry of intellectual explanations and insist on being taught the real Tantric techniques and methods of meditation that will lead them to the true experience of enlightenment.

"The advanced Tantric path," Master Fwap said with a slight sigh, as a compassionate look crossed his face, "is not for everyone. This particular truth may be hard for you to understand. You come from America, and you are a believer in the American dream of equal opportunity for all. As Buddhist monks, we share your American dream of equal opportunity for all, but Buddhism is the study of reality. Part of the reality of life is that all people may be created equally, but not all people have the same skills and abilities.

"We feel that all beings are of equal worth, whatever their level of spiritual, mental, emotional, or physical development. Studying Tantric Buddhism is like attending one of your graduate schools in the West. It is only for a person who is motivated, determined, and has a certain level of specialized intelligence. Our test to determine who has this level of commitment and intelligence is to see which seekers are fooled by the trappings and rituals of Tantric Buddhism. Spiritual seekers who think that our ocher robes, sacred books, prayer wheels, sand and rice mandala ceremonies, and other Tantric rituals are what is important, and who place little or no value on the daily practice of meditation, automatically rule themselves out from being taught the advanced tantras by a truly enlightened master. It has always been this way and it always will be this way.

"Don't misunderstand me, it is certainly true that our rituals and explanations are helpful in inspiring a seeker of truth to get to and stay on the pathway to enlightenment, but you should understand that these very rituals, practices, and ceremonies can also become a seeker of enlightenment's worst enemies."

"How is that?" My curiosity was really aroused now. I wanted an explanation. "Why would you have all of those rituals and ceremonies and all of this other Buddhist stuff if all of it might only succeed in trapping a person and preventing him from becoming enlightened?"

"Fwap!" the Oracle shouted. "He still doesn't understand our Buddhist sense of humor!"

"I will endeavor to explain it to him, O Exalted One," Master Fwap responded to the Oracle. Then the two of them started to laugh hysterically. I felt very embarrassed. I didn't know if I simply didn't get the joke, or whether I *was* the joke.

After their laughter had subsided, Master Fwap wiped the tears away from his eyes with the right sleeve of his ocher robe and resumed his explanation.

"Buddhists think that everything is funny. This may be hard for you to grasp, because you come from the West, where you have a very different concept of humor. For us, life is funny because it cannot be understood. I know this sounds contradictory, but I will explain to you what I mean, which, of course you realize is yet another ruse on my part to weave you further into one of our Tantric Buddhist tapestries of intellectual understanding."

Before I had a chance to interrupt or even contradict him, he continued. "When you look at life you see beauty and ugliness, hate and love, suffering and pleasure, truth and illusion, and salvation and redemption. As Tantric Buddhist monks we don't believe in any of those things at all. We simply pretend to believe in them when we are around people who have faith in those types of concepts."

"Isn't that lying?"

"No," he gently remarked, "it is just an expression of our Buddhist courtesy. Buddhist etiquette is very complicated. We would consider it very discourteous to tell an individual something that they didn't want to hear, which might then upset their concepts of life. In doing so it might cause them to experience pain and suffering.

"The point of Buddhist teaching," he continued, "is to help a person rise above their pain. Most individuals are so attached to their preconceived views and notions of life and enlightenment that if we were to confront them with the simple truth about enlightenment, their mind's view of the world might be destroyed and they would be intellectually, emotionally, and spiritually devastated. In other words, our explanation would not explain anything at all about enlightenment, since explanations can't. It would only take away the slight happiness that their current illusions about enlightenment already give them."

Master Fwap paused for a few moments and looked into my eyes. He then bowed slightly to me and started to speak again. "I see that you still don't understand our Tantric Buddhist sense of humor, so let me provide you with an analogy from your own culture that may help clarify this point for you.

"You have a tradition in the West of telling most young children that there is a being called Santa Claus, who comes into their houses on Christmas Eve and leaves presents for them. You tell children this because it makes them happy. Naturally, at a certain age children come to realize that there is no Santa Claus. Eventually, they find out that it was simply their parents who were putting out the presents for them while they slept, dreaming peacefully of Santa Claus on Christmas Eve.

"Now, why do you tell children this, when later they find out that Santa Claus was only a hoax? Wouldn't it be better just to tell children from the beginning that the Christmas presents they received were really from their parents?"

"Well, no. I mean, it was great for me when I was a kid to believe in Santa Claus. I would excitedly rush down the stairs on Christmas morning to discover what Santa Claus had left for me. My parents even left cookies out for him, and I would always find them half eaten. It was only when I was older that I discovered that my parents were munching out on the cookies after I went to bed on Christmas Eve, so that I would think on Christmas morning that Santa Claus had eaten some of them."

"When you found out that there was, in truth, no Santa Claus, did you experience severe mental trauma? Were you mad at your parents for having lied to you? Did you lose your faith in them or in life?"

As I was about to answer him, the Oracle interjected, "And if you were ever to have children, would you tell them that there was a Santa Claus?"

I could think of nothing to say in response to their questions. For some reason my mind went totally blank.

Master Fwap spoke up and answered his and the Oracle's questions for me. "Believing in Santa Claus as a child made you very happy, and later when you learned that there was no real Santa Claus, you were not traumatized. And yes, if you ever had children—which by the way you won't because it is not your karma to do so in this lifetime—of course you would tell them that there was a Santa Claus, because you would want them to experience the same happiness that you had when you were a child.

"Part of being a parent is protecting your children from the harsh realities of life until they are old enough to deal with and understand them in a positive and rational way. Part of being a Buddhist teacher of enlightenment is similar in many ways to being a responsible parent: We provide happy illusions to spiritual seekers until they are mature enough to deal with the more complex incongruities of the Tantric Buddhist pathway to enlightenment."

"You want the truth to be straightforward, don't you?" the Oracle asked me. "Well," he responded, again answering his own question, "I am afraid it's not!"

"Yes," Master Fwap agreed. "Truth is not straightforward, at least not the truth of enlightenment. It is the simplest thing in the world, and yet it is also the most complicated of all things.

"Try to understand," Master Fwap continued in a soothing tone of voice, "truth and enlightenment are not simply understandings of life; they are metaphysical journeys, actual experiences that your spirit has from moment to moment as it passes through eternity. To understand this, or to help get you from the 'understanding' of enlightenment to the experience, knowledge, and realization of enlightenment, is why the disembodied master posed a riddle for you to solve on top of that lone snow- and ice-covered Himalayan peak. He saw that you were ready to go beyond the child's view of enlightenment and that your power was strong enough to undertake the journey to have the actual experience of enlightenment. That journey, for you, is to solve the riddle of the missing dimensions. That is your test.

"The Oracle and I will do our best to help you solve the riddle and subsequently attain enlightenment. But we will also do our best to give you easy ways out—from time to time—so that you can keep your happy illusions, if you like, and believe that you've actually solved the riddle, when in truth you haven't. You will never know from either of us whether you have actually solved the riddle. Out of Buddhist courtesy, we will always tell you only what you want to hear.

"If you persist, and if your power is strong enough, you will break through the tapestry of Tantric Buddhist illusions that we are going to weave for you, and you will succeed in solving the riddle directly."

"Master Fwap," I complained, "how will I know whether I have solved the riddle of the missing dimensions if you and the Oracle won't tell me? It doesn't seem fair."

"You will know," Master Fwap said in a gentle tone of voice, "by the journey of your life. If you succeed in solving the riddle, then you will return to the West, and one day, in this lifetime, you will become enlightened. You will be surprised if and when you do, because you will discover that enlightenment is not at all what you 'thought' it was going to be.

"It is what it is," he continued as a small, poignant smile stole across his face. "Without a doubt, if you do become enlightened, no one in the West will really believe that you are. Those people have enough trouble believing that the Oracle and I, and other enlightened Buddhist, Hindu, and Taoist masters, are genuine, because they already have firmly established, unrealistic ideas and attitudes about how really enlightened masters should speak and behave.

"So if they can't accept us and our ways and words, because we don't fit into their cookie-cutter formulas for how enlightened beings should be, how can they possibly accept one of their own—a Caucasian—who doesn't fit their mental description of the way an enlightened person should speak and act and look? At least we are aged Orientals who dress in ocher robes, lead compact lives, and perform yogic rituals. But you, a blond American snowboarder?

"Even if you manage to solve the riddle, and then practice the advanced Tantric methods and regain your past-life enlightenment in this incarnation, everyone in both the West and the East—with the exception of other enlightened masters who can see past your

142

body's surface and into the depths of your inner being—will assume that you are a fraud. What else could they possibly believe? Think of it this way: They all still want Santa Claus, not reality, even though they claim the opposite."

"There is nothing wrong with that," the Oracle chimed in. "If you are enlightened, you won't care what people think about you. That's part of becoming enlightened. Once you have become truly enlightened, the opinions of others no longer matter to you. You know that your only true friend is the dharma."

"If you solve the riddle of the missing dimensions, and then faithfully practice the advanced Tantric meditation techniques and methods that the Oracle and I will teach you, you will become enlightened. After that, know that you will be ridiculed, and everyone will think that you are a charlatan! Instead of learning the true ways of enlightenment from you, they will all run to the unenlightened teachers who have only a conceptual understanding of enlightenment but who talk and act in such a way as to fit into their preconceived notions of how an enlightened person should appear, speak, and behave."

"Why don't people in the East believe that you and the Oracle, and other truly enlightened masters who live here, are real? Growing up in a Buddhist culture, shouldn't they be able to distinguish an enlightened master from a fake?"

"Not really," Master Fwap replied. "People are generally the same, wherever they are from. They don't, as a rule, like incongruities and anomalies. When something doesn't make sense to them they usually prefer not to deal with it rather than engage themselves in the hard work of reaching a new level of consciousness, from which they could understand and benefit from something that is both physically incongruous and cosmically complicated!

"If a master makes the practices, truths, and discussions of enlightenment simple, keeps them linear and easy to grasp intellectually, and behaves according to people's preconceived ideas of how 'holy' people should act, they are applauded and warmly accepted. But in reality almost all enlightened masters act and speak in ways that contradict the stereotypical ideas that your average person has. As you may get to see in this incarnation, enlightenment itself is not at all like what you currently imagine it to be. Being an enlightened master will not be anything like you currently imagine it to be either."

"Explain this just a little more for me, would you, Master Fwap? I'm still a little confused by all of this."

"Look at it this way," he replied. "Most people think enlightened masters aren't human. They think that we sit around in meditation all day, that we are extremely passive and always willing to 'turn the other cheek,' instead of being the strong and aggressive beings that we truly are. The mass of humanity believes that our outer behavior should be 'religious' in nature, and that all of our discussions about enlightenment should be logical and clear.

"But most real enlightened masters are exactly the opposite," Master Fwap continued to explain. "They are all true characters! They often appear to be half crazy, speak in riddles, and engage in pursuits that are not particularly puritanical. That is part and parcel of being enlightened; you have transcended space and time, and gone beyond the stereotypical trap of 'masterhood.'"

"What is this trap of masterhood?" I inquired.

"When an individual reaches a certain level in the advanced practice of yoga, he normally attains powers, understandings, and abilities that are far beyond those of mortal men and women. When average people see an advanced practitioner of yoga displaying their knowledge and powers, or intellectually sharing some of their advanced understandings of life, they immediately bow, scrape, and prostrate themselves before them.

"Power and ego are the primary obstacles to enlightenment. It's another one of our Buddhist riddles: You need occult power in order to attain enlightenment, but you can easily become addicted to occult power and the boost that it gives to your ego. If that happens, instead of transcending your ego, you get even more stuck in it than you were before you began to meditate. You willfully exchange the admiration and applause of others for your accomplishments in the advanced practices and stop advancing along the path to true enlightenment. Trust me, this happens to yogis and yoginis all of the time, isn't that right, Master Oracle?"

The Oracle nodded his head voraciously in agreement with what Master Fwap had just said.

"So, most persons who reach the verge of true enlightenment get stuck in this trap of masterhood. It is a tough trap to overcome. You can't understand any of this until you have the ability to perform miracles and know how the admiration of the crowd after you perform such a deed can be so seductive.

"It takes a great amount of willpower and purity to overcome the trap of masterhood. It's similar to the trap of wealth. If you have always been poor and have come to accept poverty as your lot in life, it is, as you would say, no big deal. But once you have become rich, powerful, or famous, even though these things in and of themselves do not create happiness, once you've had or experienced them, you will cling to any of those traps as if your life depended on them.

"The trap of masterhood is ego. It is your ego that is the cause of unhappiness and suffering in your life. It creates a partition between you and the joy and ecstasy of enlightenment. In the beginning, a seeker on the pathway to enlightenment realizes this truth and practices meditation to rise above the ego or false sense of self so they can experience the freedom and ecstasy of enlightened states of consciousness.

"As most seekers of the truth become more powerful in their yoga, they transcend their old human egos and trade them in for the egos of masterhood. They will say and do what the crowds want, because they have become addicted to admiration. Their new 'master's' ego blossoms, and suddenly instead of their egos becoming transparent, they think they know more than most of the people around them do about the inner workings of the cosmos. They come to think, now that they can impress the crowds with their erudite explanations of the meaning of life and enlightenment, and can also perform a few *siddhas*—what you would call miracles—that they have become better than the people around them.

"They now become stuck in the quicksand of their attachment to their new powers, understandings, and the approval of the crowds. As a consequence, they will not evolve any further toward enlightenment."

"You must try to understand, hard though it may be, that from our point of view we don't consider becoming enlightened a special attainment; it is simply an unusual attainment," the Oracle added.

"We don't feel that an enlightened person is better or worse than anyone else: They are everyone else. Through their countless births and deaths, they have walked through the infinite corridors of existence, experiencing every different aspect of existence. For whatever reason, one day they wanted to go beyond experiencing existence, to becoming existence itself.

"The potentially enlightened one started to walk down the corridors of the inner world that lead to enlightenment, engaging in the proper meditation practices and studying with enlightened

146

masters. They purified themselves through contemplation, hard work, and selfless giving. They made their minds as hard and bright and multifaceted as a diamond, through hundreds of incarnations of yogic practice. They fought and won the long, hard, and silent battles to overcome their ego, attachments, and aversions. It is only a rare soul who has this degree of perseverance.

"And once they have reached the border of enlightenment, they encounter a series of very subtle traps that all of us must overcome to reach the shores of nirvanic enlightenment. The most difficult of these traps is the trap of masterhood. These are the same obstacles that every practitioner of the pathway to enlightenment successfully dealt with and overcame in their previous struggles, but now they have to deal with the same traps of ego, attachment, and aversion but in much more subtle and sophisticated forms. The trap of masterhood is one of those forms, but there are several others.

"So," the Oracle said in summation, "the trick is to keep your eye on enlightenment, and, once you have found a truly enlightened master, always to do what they say—particularly when it doesn't make any sense to you."

"Why particularly then, Master Oracle?" I asked.

"Well," he replied with a laugh, "since enlightenment and the advanced practices that lead to it lie beyond logic, you have to stop making sense in order to start making sense on a more advanced level. Now as an enlightened master, what might appear sensible to you may seem completely contradictory to someone who has not yet attained enlightenment.

"Enlightened masters live in a world of complete innocence; they have transcended their egos and have gone beyond dimensionality. While they may still incarnate and have physical bodies, their inner attention is always focused on nirvana. This world as we know it is simply a playground for them."

"Let me see if I understand by putting it into snowboarding terms. When you start to study snowboarding, you learn and practice all of the techniques from the best boarders, until you have them down. If you then get good enough, you can break a lot of the rules you had to follow at the beginning. You move up to a higher level of snowboarding—where the old rules simply don't apply to you anymore, and new ones do. Beginning and intermediate snowboarders at that point would look at what you were doing and think you were nuts and out of control, because your control becomes so excellent that it's undetectable except to another world-class snowboarder's eyes. You can pull off radical things that would be unsafe for others, just because you are a world-class snowboarder. Is that more or less right?" I asked.

"The boy has a basic understanding, Fwap," the Oracle dryly remarked. "Perhaps he's not completely unteachable."

Master Fwap and the Oracle then laughed together, sharing some private joke that I didn't get, after which they were silent for several minutes.

Master Fwap then asked me, "So now do you understand our Buddhist sense of humor? Naturally, like anything in advanced Buddhist practice, it cannot be explained, but you can draw inferences and come to deeper understandings, if you allow your mind to absorb what we tell you without analyzing it to death or trying to make it into an all-encompassing, logical paradigm, which somehow must always work and be true in all places, in all cases, and at all times.

"Here in the East," he continued, "we see the seekers of enlightenment gather by the tens of thousands around the unenlightened teachers who have only a conceptual understanding of enlightenment and who act and speak in a way that fits into the

Eastern people's preconceived notions of how masters should act and speak.

"The Oracle and I, and other enlightened masters, are generally ignored. It should be this way. There is nothing wrong with it. If the seekers of enlightenment were truly ready for the actual training and experience of enlightenment, they would leave the masters who have only an intellectual understanding and not rest until they found us, or someone like us who is truly enlightened and could show them the more advanced mysteries of the path.

"This is our Buddhist sense of humor," Master Fwap said in summation. "It is a happy humor, it is not based on meanness. We do not find the pain and misfortune of others funny, although we do find our own pain and misfortunes funny.

"We watch the seekers of enlightenment run to their 'spiritual' Santa Clauses, because that is what they really need at this point in their evolution. We deal with the few who are ready to go beyond the support structures and illusions of basic Buddhism, who are mentally prepared to embrace the more incongruous advanced teachings and practices of Tantric Buddhism. Those are the few who progress beyond samsara—illusion—and on to enlightenment. Everything is as it should be.

"In our Buddhist sense of humor we have a happy sense of the ironic sides of life. Everything is an illusion, and all illusions have their purposes. From our complex Tantric Buddhist viewpoint, therefore, there are no real illusions at all. Illusions are steps along the path, if you see what I mean."

I could think of nothing to say.

The Oracle suddenly stood up, bowed to me, and said, "O future enlightened one, know that all of this means nothing. There is nothing to mean, nothing to know, no one to mean it, and no

149

one to know it. And," he said with a chuckle, "if you believe this one, we'll tell you another!"

The Oracle then collapsed on the floor in spasms of laughter. I looked nervously over at Master Fwap, only to see that he was cracking up too. At first I felt totally frustrated because I assumed they were laughing at my lack of understanding, but after a few minutes of their happy laughter, my sense of frustration, much to my surprise, suddenly vanished.

Their laughter became infectious. After a few more minutes, I was laughing along with the both of them, as hard as they were! Suddenly everything seemed funny to me, and I felt happy and free. It was as if I had suddenly—without knowing how or why—been liberated from some kind of internal heaviness that I had been carrying around deep inside of myself, without even knowing that I was carrying it around.

As I was laughing along with Master Fwap and the Oracle I had no idea why I was really laughing. It didn't seem to matter, though, so I just kept laughing on and on until tears were streaming down my face.

After our laughter had subsided, I looked at Master Fwap and the Oracle. Both of their eyes were shining with an intensity that was so bright that I could hardly look back at them. They didn't have to explain anything more to me, though; I was content with the knowledge that I didn't understand their intellectual explanations, or need to.

13

THE TAO OF SNOW

For four days Master Fwap, the Oracle, and I had been trekking our way through and across the winding trails that wove their way between the majestic Anapurna Himalayas. We had crossed countless lofty snow-crested summit passes and also walked in the deep shadows and pin-drop silence of their hidden valleys. Most of our time had been spent trekking without conversation. Speech didn't seem appropriate. The sheer magnitude and sharp, stark beauty of the Anapurna Himalayas would have been degraded by conversations.

I had never seen mountains that were this beautiful. The stone- and snow-faced Anapurna Himalayas jutted straight up and disappeared into a cerulean blue sky that was broken at varying altitudes by different-colored layers of puffy clouds. Each morning and evening, as the vivid colorations of the Himalayan sunrises and sunsets flooded the skies and clouds, the Anapurna peaks were tinted with light pink, red, cyan, and deep purplish hues and shadows.

Each day of our journey I was simply more overwhelmed by the sights that greeted my eyes. The only other places that I had visited on earth that even remotely resembled the breathtaking beauty of the Anapurna Himalayas were areas along the lake in

Kashmir and the stately majestic views of the Matterhorn that one gets in Zermatt, Switzerland.

On the fourth day of our journey, while resting on the western side of a prayer flag–covered pass, my mind was suddenly flooded with questions about enlightenment. For the first time in my life I really wanted to know more about the subject of Buddhist self-realization. I wanted to know how to meditate well, how many other dimensions there really were, what they were like, how karma and reincarnation worked, and what nirvana was all about.

I asked Master Fwap and the Oracle why I had suddenly become so unexpectedly interested in subjects that, up until that moment, I had heavily resisted studying.

"It is because of those who have traversed these paths before us," Master Fwap explained, as the three of us sat facing each other in a tightly knit circle while basking in the late afternoon amber Himalayan sunlight.

"What do you mean by that?"

"As you have seen with your own eyes, prayer flags are hung along and around the tops of the passes we have been crossing together during the course of our trek these last several days. These flags have been inscribed with Sanskrit prayers by the Nepalese and Tibetan people who have walked here before us on their pilgrimages to and from the holy places of power and enlightenment that lie deep within caves that are hidden in these sacred mountains.

"It is the Buddhist and Hindu pilgrims' belief," he continued in a reverential tone of voice, "that as their prayer flags, which they have placed along these mountain passes, flutter in the winds that flow through the Himalayas, the prayers that they have written on them are being said over and over, by the flags themselves.

"In addition, they believe that the Himalayan winds that move their flags actually carry their prayers to the gods and other beings that exist in higher dimensional planes."

"How's that? The flags are just made of cloth, and the prayers on them are written in ink. How can pieces of cloth that are covered with ink possibly say prayers to the gods for the people who put them there?"

"What you see with your eyes and feel with your heart are not always the same, would you agree?" Master Fwap asked me with a tone of unexpected urgency in his voice.

"Yes, that's true," I automatically responded.

"Well," he continued, "that is the case with the prayer flags that Buddhist pilgrims place around and over the Himalayan mountain passes. Yes, I agree with you, that on the surface their prayer flags are made only of ink and cloth. How could they possibly pray? Flags aren't living beings, and only living beings can pray, isn't that correct, from your point of view?"

"Yes," I tentatively responded. I had the feeling that I was a thread that was about to be woven into another one of Master Fwap's Tantric Buddhist tapestries of illusion.

"If that is your point of view, you would be making a great mistake," he remarked. "The prayer flags are alive—isn't that correct, O great Oracle of Nepal?"

The Oracle quickly and rapidly nodded his head three times in agreement with Master Fwap's statement.

"As you can plainly see," Master Fwap casually remarked as he stretched out and relaxed his arms against the rough ground behind him, "the Oracle agrees with me: The flags are alive, and they are praying. The winds that whip across the Himalayan passes carry the pilgrims' prayers into forever," he said with complete certainty.

"Oh, come on, Master Fwap, you must be kidding. Pieces of cloth can't pray," I immediately snapped back at him.

"Oh, yes they can," he said with a gentle voice.

"Oh, yes they can," echoed the Oracle, in a deep and somber tone of voice.

"No they can't!" I said defiantly. "I mean, really, after all we have been through, Master Fwap, I'm open to learning new things about Buddhism and the universe—but pieces of cloth that are alive and say prayers for the pilgrims who put them there? That's straight out of a Disney movie. You guys must be kidding me."

"Oh, no we're not," said Master Fwap with certainty.

"Oh, no we're not," chimed in the Oracle.

"Well then, explain it to me!" I demanded in frustration.

"O, great Oracle of Nepal," Master Fwap began, "would you be so kind as to enlighten our young American disciple as to how it is possible for inanimate prayer flags to say real prayers to the gods?"

In response to Master Fwap's question, the Oracle leaped to his feet and then jumped up into the air. I watched his body move in an upward arc and halt, and then as I waited for him to start to fall and hit the ground, to my utter and total amazement, the Oracle didn't come down! Instead he just hung there, suspended in the air by some invisible power, levitating his body, about three feet from the ground, right in front of me!

"Oh, yes they can," Master Fwap said again.

"Oh, yes they can," the levitating Oracle agreed, with a Cheshire Cat grin right out of *Alice in Wonderland* plastered across his face.

As I watched with awe, the Oracle continued to hover, suspended magically in the air. I was seriously speechless. Then, as he continued to levitate smoothly, several feet above the ground, he asked me the following question: "How do you keep an idiot in suspense?"

I was so freaked out by the fact that he was just hanging comfortably in the air, levitating several feet in front of me, that it took me a couple of moments before I was able to stammer out my response: "I don't know, Master Oracle, how do you keep an idiot in suspense? I am completely clueless."

Looking down upon me, from his levitating height, he responded, "I'll tell you tomorrow."

Master Fwap and the Oracle immediately burst into long peals of howling laughter. After their laughter had finally subsided, the levitating Oracle stretched out both of his arms in either direction as far as he could. He made some kind of a whooshing sound with his breath, and two bright white beams of light shot out from the palms of his hands and into the air and sky around him.

As I watched in awe, the light that continued to flow out from the palms of his hands illuminated the surrounding mountains, making them look viscous and surreal, as if they were some kind of vibrating wavy papier-mâché.

I rubbed my eyes to try and adjust them, but it didn't make any difference at all. I could still distinctly see the Oracle's levitating body lighting up and transforming the mountains that surrounded us.

The Oracle then brought down his arms and clapped his hands loudly together three times. His body gently, silently, and gracefully descended to the earth.

The Oracle was now standing in front of me, with both of his feet firmly planted on the ground. I heard Master Fwap's voice talking to me, but it sounded very distant and faded, as if it were coming from very far away. I couldn't discern whatever it was that he was saying to me.

Then my eyes closed of their own accord and I stopped thinking. My mind became completely still; the only thing I was aware of was the distant sound of the Himalayan wind as it rushed over the pass we had just crossed.

An immeasurable amount of time passed. I might have been on the ground with my eyes closed for a few moments or forever, I couldn't tell the difference. Without realizing it, I had entered into some kind of tranced-out state, in which time didn't exist the way that it normally did. Everything felt momentary and yet at the same time every moment seemed like an eternity.

When I opened my eyes, I saw Master Fwap and the Oracle sitting very near me, just as they had been before the Oracle had leaped into the air and levitated. Their eyes were wide open as they both intently watched me.

Master Fwap started to speak, and this time I had no trouble understanding his words: "The prayer flags are alive with the beliefs and prayers of the Buddhist pilgrims who placed them across these passes. I do not mean this metaphorically; in all actuality they have been fully animated by the power of the pilgrims' auras."

"How can that be, Master Fwap?" I heard myself asking.

"Perhaps you would better understand this if we first discussed the Tao of snow," he replied.

"What is the Tao of snow?"

"Let's start with a definition. Tao is a Chinese word that is very hard to translate into English, because it has so many different meanings."

"What are some of them?" I inquired with interest. I had heard the word "Tao" used before by my kung fu master back in the United States, but I had never really understood what he meant by it.

"Well," he began, "Tao means the way something is or hap-

156

pens; it would also be equally correct to say that Tao means the movement of life. The word also suggests that there are correct and incorrect attitudes and appropriate and inappropriate ways to be and act in different situations.

"Tao is often initially easier to understand as an image," he continued to explain. "In the East, water is most often used as the symbol for Tao. Water is something that has no particular form. It assumes the shape of any vessel that it is placed into. Tao is also seen as perennial movement. Since life is always in motion, so is Tao.

"Now, there are many different ways to move. As a snow-boarder I am sure you are more aware of this than most people are."

"Yes, but what does that have to do with Tao?"

"Well," he responded after several moments of silence, "think about movement for a moment. All motions are not the same; some are appropriate and some are not. Appropriate motions are the motions that are the most efficient: You might say that they work out the best, or that they require less energy to effect. Inappropriate motions are those that require more work and use up energy unnecessarily because they are inefficient.

"If you stand back, metaphorically speaking," he continued, "and look at the vast panorama of existence, you will see that the universe is completely efficient. Nothing is ever wasted. Life recycles itself in innumerable ways out of itself, always creating new forms out of its older forms.

"Now let us get more specific and look at the movement of water in a stream as an example of Tao," he continued to elucidate. "When water is flowing through a riverbed and it encounters an enormous rock, it naturally flows around the rock, instead of flowing over it. It is easier for it to do so.

"But don't underestimate the power of water! Even though a rock may be very large and solid, while water is very liquid and soft, if the water flows around the rock long enough, it begins to wear the rock down, in spite of the water's softness and the rock's apparent hardness. As time passes, the softness of the water will start to consume the hardness of the rock; eventually the rock will be completely worn away, and the river's water will flow freely where once the huge rock blocked its pathway.

"So Tao is a word that signifies a way or a series of approaches to mental, physical, emotional, and spiritual situations that we encounter as we go through life. Think of the relationship between the water and the rock.

"As Buddhists, we believe that each human being has the ability to make a choice: to follow the indirect ways of Tao or to approach life in a head-on manner, as most people do.

"When the idea of Tao as a method for living and problem solving is explained to most people, their first reaction is that Tao seems like a very weak or passive way to approach things. But if you wish to produce long-term or profound effects within or around yourself, the way of Tao is the supreme method for doing so."

I interrupted, "One of my martial arts teachers in kung fu talked to me in class about Tao. But it was related to fighting. He explained that trying to punch and kick your way to victory wasn't always the best approach for dealing with extreme, confrontational situations. It was often better to use the motion and power of your opponents to defeat them, he said. Instead of blocking a punch with your arm, and maybe getting your arm bruised or broken if your opponent was skillful, he showed us how to grab our opponent's moving arm, put a wrist lock on it, and spin our body and rotate with the motion of our attacker's punch.

"By flowing with our opponent's attack, instead of directly opposing it, we would be able to avoid injury and also use the power of our attacker's energy to defeat them. We could do all of this without using up as much of our energy as we would if we responded with a series of counterattacks and opposing movements—which he told us would not only tire us out but also make us more vulnerable, if we were fighting either an experienced opponent or multiple opponents. It seems to me that you are describing a similar principle when you refer to Tao, Master Fwap."

"Exactly, that's it. You can deal with the situations in life head-on and wear yourself out, or you can approach them at an angle and let them wear themselves out. Back to my water and rock analogy," Master Fwap replied, slowly and carefully enunciating each word as he spoke it.

"I think I'm beginning to understand. Maybe another example would help."

"I am sure that you have had similar experiences in snowboarding," he continued. "There are harder ways to snowboard, where you don't go with the flow of the snow, and there are easier ways to snowboard, where you flow with the snow. Isn't that true?"

"Definitely. That is how you can tell a good snowboarder from a bad snowboarder. A good snowboarder lets the gravity of the mountain take him down it. A bad snowboarder is always fighting against the gravity of the mountain and uses up too much of their power straining with their leg muscles and pushing too hard against their board. At the end of a run they are tired because they kept moving their body against the mountain's energy, instead of moving with the mountain's energy.

"When you snowboard down a slope well, you shouldn't really feel tired. If anything, you should feel better and have more energy afterward than you did before you began; that's part of what makes snowboarding such an outstanding sport.

"It looks completely different when you are watching it. It's like high diving. When you watch really good divers at the Olympics, no matter how many spins in the air they do during their dive, when then enter the water they leave almost no splash or wake. Bad divers don't hit the water as cleanly, and there is a lot of splash.

"It's really the same with snowboarding. When you watch an outrageous boarder board, they don't kick up much snow, even when they are trick riding or high jumping. The angle they land on is so even that the snow is hardly even disturbed."

"That is precisely what I was referring to when I was talking about taking an angular approach to life, rather then dealing with situations head-on," Master Fwap responded. "As Buddhist monks we are trained to approach different situations that we encounter in our inner and outer lives, and that includes problem solving, in angular ways, ways that are somewhat analogous to your diving and snowboarding metaphors."

"What is an angular approach to problem solving like? Can you give me another explanation that I can relate to?"

"It's easy to understand," he said with a knowing smile. "When your head hurts from trying to solve a problem and you are filled with frustration, you are trying to tackle the problem head-on. When the problem seems to solve itself or just disappears on its own, and you find the experience of solving it enjoyable, you have used an angular approach."

"I'm not sure if I get it," I replied. "Can you define the angular approach to living and problem solving for me in a more concrete way?"

"Sure. Let us use mathematics to understand this. Suppose you are trying to solve an equation, and no matter how many times you factor it, you can't get your equation to balance properly. Now, the average person will simply become frustrated. They will find fault with themselves or the equation and either give up in anger or depression. If they are headstrong, they will just keep mentally pounding away at the equation, angrily looking for a proper solution to it.

"The chances that they will solve a difficult equation this way are minimal," he explained. "They may factor and refactor the equation over and over again, but if they don't find a different angle to view the equation from, they will only be bringing the same mind-set back to the equation again and again. If their previous mind-set wasn't able to factor the equation initially, why would it be able to later?

"Taking the angular approach to problem solving means that you would forget about the equation for a while and go and do something else. Later, in a different frame of mind, you might see the equation in an entirely new light. Then with this new frame of mind you would find it easier and more enjoyable to solve."

"What would change a person's frame of mind that much? Wouldn't the person just be goofing off and running away from the problem he is trying to solve?" I asked, my interest in our conversation gradually growing.

"It could be, but that would not be employing the Taoistic angular method of problem solving. You see, my young American friend, everything in life does not have to be as complicated as you sometimes make it. When you are in a clear mental state, things are relatively easy and uncomplicated to understand and deal with. When, however, you are in a confused or highly emotional state of mind, even the easiest things in life can seem overly complicated and impossible to solve or understand.

"So, getting back to your question," Master Fwap continued, "an angular approach to problem solving involves the use of your second attention. By allowing your second attention to move your mind to a different and higher nodal point, you gain a more advanced way to problem-solve."

"How do you use your second attention?"

"Why, you meditate, of course!" The Oracle shouted out with a laugh.

"That's right," agreed Master Fwap.

"That's right," the Oracle echoed.

"But how is meditating on an equation going to cause me to solve it, or any other problem, for that matter? As I meditated on it, wouldn't I just be thinking even more about the equation or the problem and get even more wrapped up and frustrated by it?"

"No," Master Fwap replied simply.

"Knowing you, you might!" the Oracle said with a quick laugh.

"The true answer to your question," Master Fwap said, as he smoothly resumed his explanation, "is to understand how meditation enables you to alter the nodal points of perception within your mind."

"I think that this might be easier for me to understand if you would first explain to me what a nodal point of perception is."

"A nodal point of perception is the view that you have of life at any given moment in time and space. If you were able to see into your second attention, as the Oracle and I can, you would see that you actually have countless nodal points within your nonphysical mind, deep within your second attention's perceptual field.

"Most people have access to only one or two of these nodal points of perception," he continued. "Persons whom most people refer to as geniuses have access to perhaps a half dozen or so of their nodal points of perception.

"In reality, there are an infinite number of nodal points of

162

perception hidden within your second attention. In and through the practice of meditation, you can learn about and experience many or all of these nodal points. When you are very skillful in yoga, you can even consciously change nodal points at will, selecting the proper nodal point for whatever life situation or problem you currently need to deal with or solve."

"I don't mean to sound dumb, but I still don't get how meditating on a particular problem is any different from sitting around and thinking about it. What's the difference?"

"The only difficulty you are having with this is that you lack a clear understanding of what meditation truly is. When I say that you should meditate on a problem in order to solve it, I mean the opposite of what you think I mean."

"How's that?"

"Okay, relax your mind for a moment. Now instead of trying to grasp what I am saying, just let my words flow into your second attention. Don't try to understand or analyze them, and perhaps you will comprehend my explanation without my having to explain it to you."

"The reason you are having a problem understanding this is that you are seeing all of this as a problem that you must solve to begin with," the Oracle casually remarked.

"The Oracle is right," Master Fwap said with complete conviction. "You are trying too hard to understand, and therefore you are blocking your ability to understand. Don't ask any more questions for a few minutes. Just sit back and relax, and let my explanation become your understanding."

"Okay, I'll try," I replied, without much confidence in my voice.

"It's so easy," Master Fwap said in an uncharacteristically strong tone of voice. "Whenever you meditate on a problem you need to deal with or solve, don't think about it at all. In meditation you stop all of your thoughts instead. Additional thought, analysis, or speculation on what appears to be an insoluble problem for you only drains and frustrates you. You have a phrase in your English language, and even though it is uncharacteristically Buddhist in flavor, I think if I use it you will immediately understand the point: There is more than one way to skin a cat."

"Yes, that's a common phrase we use in America."

"So by not thinking about a problem, and meditating on emptiness instead, you fill your mind with more energy," he continued. "This additional psychic energy will then enable your conscious mind to call on or activate the higher nodal points in your second attention. After meditating, without knowing or understanding how your mind has managed it, the answer to the problem you are trying to solve will just come to you. That is all there is to it."

"Okay, I've got that, but what does all of this have to do with the Tao of snow? I think I understand what you are talking about now in terms of problem solving and meditating. By meditating, I can change my current state of mind into a higher state of mind. In this higher state of mind, which you refer to as a higher nodal point of perception, I can see the problem differently and more clearly and from what you refer to as a different angle, and then I can come up with an answer that is correct."

"Your boy's got it!" The Oracle shouted in mock surprise.

"Yes, that is correct," Master Fwap said in a slow and patient tone of voice. "Now the true understanding of the Tao of snow, like solving your next problem—finding the secret of the missing dimensions—is just a little bit more cosmically complicated."

"Master Fwap, I think I am really starting to understand all of this," I said. A tone of excitement began to creep into my voice.

"Beware of understandings," warned the Oracle. "Stick with

knowing nothing. When you know nothing, you will understand everything."

"That's correct," Master Fwap said as a tone of approval warmed the sound of his voice. "Don't try to reason this all out. Just let my explanations flow into your second attention, without analyzing or thinking about them, and after that everything will become perfectly clear to you."

"But wait, you said that the Tao of snow and the secret of the missing dimensions are even more complicated. If that is the case, how will this method work on something more advanced?"

"The way to simplify a problem is by simplifying yourself," the Oracle flatly stated.

"What the Oracle says is, of course, true," Master Fwap agreed. "Most people try to solve or simplify a problem by working on their approach to it. A Buddhist monk occasionally does that, but usually a monk uses an angular, nonconceptual approach to solving or simplifying a complex problem or situation. Instead of simplifying or solving the problem or situation, if that can't easily be done in a straightforward and logical manner, a Buddhist monk is trained to temporarily ignore the problem or situation and instead work on simplifying and solving himself.

"Having done so, and having accordingly reached a deeper level of clarity—which is a new view from a higher nodal point within his second attention—he returns to his previously 'insoluble' problem or situation. From the perspective of the new mental state he has gained by changing himself, the answer becomes immediately apparent to him."

"In short," the Oracle said in summation, "we believe as Buddhist monks that the best way to approach life's complexities and answer its most difficult questions is by finding the answers— through the vehicle of meditation—within our own minds.

"We go deep within, in order to understand how to live and act in the world around us. We use the outer knowledge that we have learned from others or gained through our personal experiences, but we find that complicated situations are easier to solve by accessing the different nodal points within our second attention."

"I still don't see what this has to do with the Tao of snow. How does knowledge of the Tao of snow answer my original question: Why have I suddenly become so interested in the subject of enlightenment since we have been trekking around and over the Anapurna Himalayas, when before we came here my primary interests were snowboarding, rock and roll, martial arts, and sex?

"All of the Buddhist principles that both of you have been kind enough to try and teach me have gotten my interest only because Master Fwap convinced me on our first journeys together that learning Buddhism would improve my snowboarding technique."

"The answer to both of your questions is the same," Master Fwap replied. "Let me explain, but as before, no more questions. Just relax and let my answer flow into your second attention; don't try to reason it out or make sense of it. Just let my answer be enough for you now, without further questioning or explanation.

"At some point in your future, you will have done enough meditation to find the right nodal point. At that time the explanation I am about to give to you will explain everything, without your having to understand it.

"Now the Tao of snow is as follows," he continued in a very soft and rhythmic tone of voice that caused me to have to listen carefully to and concentrate on each of his words. "It is emptiness. The Tao of snow is emptiness, at least initially. When snow falls from the Himalayan skies it has no particular vibration, you might say that it is empty and pure—it has no mental impressions of its own. It is like the prayer flags before the pilgrims construct them; initially they are only cloth and ink.

"After the snow falls, people walk over it on their way from one place to another. As they walk, they are holding in their minds their conscious and subconscious thoughts, emotions, hopes, fears, and expectations, along with their overall knowledge and ignorance. All of these are then amplified by the amount of personal power they have.

"We call the sum total of a person's mental state at any given time their aura," he continued. "An aura is living energy, and it affects things it touches, just as your body affects something that you physically touch. The only difference is that an aura leaves a psychic impression, which can be seen only with a person's 'psychic' eyes, while the effects on material things that you physically touch can be perceived with your physical eyes.

"Here in the Anapurna Himalayas as the Buddhist and Hindu pilgrims pray and think about enlightenment, and while they walk on these trails and cross the passes that we have been crossing, their auras impart their psychic impressions not only on the Himalayan snow but on the mountains and on the paths and passes that they traverse as well. You cannot see these impressions with your eyes, but your mind can telepathically feel them.

"So that's why when we walk here, your mind is filled with their thoughts, thoughts about reincarnation, meditation, enlightenment, karma, and other metaphysical topics.

"In many of the other places you have been in the world you have been walking on 'dirty snow.' It is no longer crystal white and pure; it has become polluted by the lower desires and aversions of humankind.

"In Los Angeles, and even in Katmandu, when you walk through those streets they are filled with the psychic impressions of the people who have passed down them before you. Unlike the Anapurna trails and passes, which are frequented only by the devotees of higher spiritual dimensions, the streets you normally walk on are filled with the worldly loves, hates, desires, fears, and violence of your fellow human beings.

"In aurically polluted environments, it requires more effort to be interested in enlightenment. That is why we make pilgrimages to special caves out here, in the purity of nature, far away from the unhappy and worldly impressions of our fellow human beings.

"Now you might begin to understand how the prayer flags work," Master Fwap continued to explain with enthusiasm. "When the Buddhist and Hindu pilgrims make the flags and write their prayers on them, the energy from their auras psychically charges the auric fields of the flags. The flags become positively charged with the spiritual prayers of the people who construct them, in much the same way that you can charge up and increase the power in a battery by connecting it to an electrical charger.

"Everything in the universe affects everything else. Since everything is made up of moving particles of energy, when one energy field encounters another—or as we say in Buddhism, when auras touch—they have a more profound effect on each other than you might suppose.

"That is why it is important that you solve the riddle of the missing dimensions now. These very mountains, trails, and passes are attracting more and more tourists and mountain climbers each day, and they are rapidly becoming more aurically polluted. In a few short years," he said with a laugh, "you might have to become a scuba diver and go hundreds of feet underwater to experience what you are feeling here now. It will be the last refuge of pure aura and power on our planet, the oceans' depths. It will be the only place left that human beings have not yet polluted with their vibrations!

"So the Tao of snow," he said in a reflective tone of voice, as if he were talking to himself, "is moving with the energy of clear understanding. This understanding is attainable in places that are pure to practice meditation. Make pilgrimages to power places and places of enlightenment to recharge yourself when you find it necessary to clear your mind. If you go to places that used to be pure but are now aurically polluted, relying on their former reputation as places of power and enlightenment, you are going against the Tao of enlightenment—if enlightenment is what you seek. You are flowing against, not with, the energy of enlightenment. You are, in other words, walking on dirty snow.

"If you seek clean snow, if that is your necessity or aesthetic preference, then you must follow the Tao of clean snow and flow wherever the purest aura exists today. You can't rely on the old places of power and enlightenment anymore, as you would say in your colliquial Los Angeles language, those places are now 'lined out.' Their power has been so obscured by layers of dirty aura that they won't produce the effect that your mind, body, and spirit are seeking.

"The Tao of enlightenment is always the same and is always changing. Go with its current flow, in the here and now. Adapt and change with the world and the dharma: This has always been the cornerstone of the pathway to Buddhist enlightenment: Go with the flow of the enlightened energy and not against it."

14

Master Fwap Goes "Phat!"

We sat in silence for some time after Master Fwap had finished speaking. The Oracle and Master Fwap then abruptly stood up, as if they had sensed something at exactly the same moment that I apparently was oblivious to.

"The time has come for us to begin our journey to the cave of enlightenment. It lies hidden not too much farther from here, but we must leave at once!" the Oracle stated emphatically.

"Gather your things and we will go," Master Fwap said to me in a serious tone. "The Oracle's pronouncement is correct, of course. The 'just right' karmic moment for your journey to solve the riddle of the missing dimensions has finally arrived. Hurry, we must not miss this moment!"

After Master Fwap's and the Oracle's pronouncements, I wasted no time. I quickly retrieved my backpack and snowboard, and after shouldering them, the three of us walked forward into the unknown.

We had been hiking for several hours down a mountainside and into a valley. As we continued walking, the sun slowly began to slide behind the Anapurna Himalayas, causing us to walk into ever-darkening mountain shadows.

The air became much cooler as we descended into the valley. I was actually shivering by the time we had reached its lowest point. The trail took an unexpected upward turn, and suddenly we were hiking up an extremely stiff vertical section of the tree-lined trail.

It was near dark when we reached the top of the pass. The sun had almost finished setting, and thousands of stars were starting to shine down on us, although the moon had yet to make its appearance.

Even though we were now trekking at a much higher altitude, I felt much warmer than I had when we were in the valley below. I didn't know whether to attribute my sudden increased warmth to the exertion of hiking up an extreme vertical section of the trail, or to some unseen thermal inversion, or to a combination of both.

As time passed and the sun completely disappeared behind the stark and beautiful Anapurna Himalayas, we started to navigate our way along the trail by starlight. Master Fwap led, closely followed by the Oracle and me.

The trail we were traversing then crossed a pass, and Master Fwap led us away from the trail we had been following and onto a very narrow path that intersected with the main trail. This new path swung toward the south side of the mountain.

After about thirty minutes on this new path Master Fwap suddenly stopped. I was trying to figure out why he had stopped so abruptly, so I squinted my eyes to see if something lay ahead that was blocking our progress. I couldn't see a thing. All I could do was to wonder whether an object was blocking the way ahead, or to wonder if Master Fwap had gotten lost.

My unspoken conjecture was rapidly resolved. Master Fwap

turned and suddenly announced in a jubilant voice, "We have arrived at our most sacred destination. It is here that you will solve the riddle of the missing dimensions. Phat!"

Then Master Fwap began to walk forward very slowly. Both the Oracle and I followed him into an opening of what appeared to be a very large cave. In the blackness of the night it was difficult to see practically anything, but as best as I could tell by starlight, I surmised that the mouth of the cave was about twenty feet high.

As we entered deeper into the cave the starlight vanished, and the three of us were suddenly swallowed up by the cave's complete blackness.

Walking slowly forward, step by step, for several more minutes, I started to feel the cave's depth.

We walked in complete silence, one slow step at a time, for about five more minutes, until Master Fwap came to a halt again.

Master Fwap struck a match. I could see by the dim light of the match that we had entered a large rock and earthen cavern that had been skillfully converted into a comfortable Buddhist sanctuary.

The walls of the cave were covered with colorful *thankas* depicting meditating Buddhas and other deities in both bright and faded colors. Prayer rugs and multicolored cushions had been placed in symmetrical patterns on several different areas of the cave's earthen floor. Dozens of thick white wax candles rested in tarnished brass holders attached to the cave's walls.

Master Fwap gradually lit all of the candles along both of the cave's walls, using up several matches in the process. When he was finished and all of the candles in the cave were burning brightly, I could see the entirety of the cave.

In the candles' flickering light, I began to make a mental inventory of my new environment. I was standing about one third of the way into the cave, facing toward its back end. On the floor and slightly to my right were several small, worn brown wooden four-legged tables. On each of the tables there were dozens of ancient-looking clothbound manuscripts of varying sizes, all of which had been neatly piled in stacks.

To my left on the cave's floor, running along its opposite wall, were different types of black iron cooking utensils, a large greenish metal teapot, and a set of faded china dishes, along with some wooden eating utensils.

Toward the rear of the cave were six heavy burlap sacks, similar to those I had often seen in the open-air markets in Katmandu. Judging from their bulging appearance, and aided by their partially opened tops, I saw that they were filled with rice, barley, and other types of grains.

On the cave's floor, farther to my left, was a deep round pit. It was partially filled with some gray and white ashes and small pieces of old charred and blackened firewood.

Above the fire pit, in the cave's ceiling, was a narrow fissure that ran through a small section of the roof's rock. In the middle of the fissure there was a small round opening.

I was surprised by the quantity of artifacts that filled the cave and at the amount of effort it must have taken to carry them over the high snowy passes and steep trails from Katmandu.

As I squinted my eyes and looked back toward the rear of the cave, I noticed piles of thick Nepalese woolen blankets, sleeping pads, and a variety of Tibetan Buddhist ornaments that included three brass ceremonial *dorjes*, two long Nepalese trumpets, a number of wooden prayer wheels, and dozens of sets of prayer beads.

"Now come here and sit down and relax," Master Fwap said, interrupting my assessment process of the cave's interior.

"I will start a fire to warm us," he continued in a cheerful tone of voice. "We have traveled a long way and we should all sit and rest. Please feel free to place your pack and snowboard wherever you like."

After his pronouncement Master Fwap began softly to hum a Buddhist chant. Then, approaching the fire pit, he started to pile large pieces of wood into the pit that he obtained from a stack of wood adjacent to and directly behind the rear of the fire pit.

He then took what looked like old dried summer grass, placed it under the wood, and lit it with another match. The flames rose immediately from the dried grass and quickly set the wood on fire. The crackling and popping sounds that the wood made as it burned made me feel cozy and right at home.

The Oracle walked up to me and handed me a large white meditation cushion that had been embroidered with a red and blue dragon on it. He motioned with his right hand for me to sit down next to him near the fire.

I was engaged in what was, from my point of view, a wonderful scene. After days of trekking through the Himalayas on narrow trails, crossing over snow- and ice-covered passes, and sleeping in cold, small, simple wooden shelters that had been erected by the pilgrims who traversed the pathways between the Anapurnas on their religious journeys, I was now the occupant of what I considered to be a "five star" cave.

The three of us crowded together, soaking up as much of the fire's warmth as we could. Master Fwap made us tea from snowmelt and some kind of dried green herbs he had gotten from the rear of the cave. He combined these in the metal teapot, which he hung over the fire pit on a blackened iron rod. Then he set about boiling some of the grains in several old metal pots, placing the pots directly on top of the fire. I was absolutely famished.

The Oracle stood up and retrieved some plates from the side of the cave, along with some strange wooden eating utensils that looked like oversized bent spoons with tiny holes in them. After a while, the three of us were feasting on freshly cooked rice and barley, and drinking hot tea. If there was a nirvana, at that moment I was convinced that I had finally reached it.

After we had finished eating, and the Oracle had cleaned and put the dishes away, Master Fwap placed more wood on the fire. I found myself yawning, and I was looking forward to drifting off to sleep under some of the woolen blankets I had seen in the back of the cave. Master Fwap must have been reading my thoughts because he immediately poured me another cup of tea and then told me that it was very important that I stay awake for the next several hours—because something "very powerful" was about to happen to me.

I yawningly agreed. I was so happy at that moment not to be spending another freezing night trying to sleep in a makeshift wooden trail hut that I happily promised him that I wouldn't fall asleep, no matter how tired I was. But I must admit, his admonishment that something "powerful" was going to take place over the next few hours certainly didn't prepare me for the strange scenes I was about to witness that night in the sacred cave of enlightenment, deep in the Anapurna Himalayas.

Everything started out normally enough. First Master Fwap stood up and stretched, then the Oracle did the same. After stretching, the two of them walked around and around the cave together, saying nothing but looking very intently at the cave's walls.

I was about to ask them what they were looking for when suddenly, in the loudest voice I have ever heard him use, Master Fwap shouted "Phat!" Then he said "Phat!" again, in an even louder voice.

He started to shout "Phat! Phat! Phat! Phat." Then the Oracle started to shout "Phat!" repeatedly, along with Master Fwap, in an even louder voice.

The combined sound of their shouted "Phats" was significantly amplified by the echoing "Phats" that the cave boomed back at them. Within a few minutes the sound of the shouted and echoed "Phats" became almost deafening. My ears started to ring like they did during a rock concert.

"Phat! Phat! Phat! Phat! Phat!" they shouted intensely, over and over, as they both walked repeatedly up and down the sides of the cave. I was convinced that the two of them had come totally unglued when, without warning, they both suddenly stopped.

Turning toward me, they both started to walk over to where I was sitting dumbfounded in front of the fire. They gracefully seated themselves on either side of me, in cross-legged positions, neatly tucking their ocher robes under their legs.

After all of their shouting, the sudden silence in the cave now seemed deafening. My ears were still ringing from all of the shouted and echoed "Phats," but for some reason that I couldn't quite figure out, the silence that now filled the cave seemed even louder than their combined shouting had been.

We sat in silence for several more minutes, staring into the fire. Gradually the ringing in my ears subsided, and turning my head from side to side I closely examined first Master Fwap's expression, and then the Oracle's expression, in an attempt to figure out what they were up to.

But it was no use. They had both closed their eyes and had entered into a state of deep meditation. I assumed that I should do the same thing, and so I closed my eyes and started to practice the "Blue Sky" meditation technique I had recently read in *The Handbook for Enlightenment.*

Initially, as *The Handbook* had instructed, I began to picture a beautiful blue sky without any clouds in it. Then, as it had outlined, I imagined that my body felt very light, as if it were floating.

I continued to practice the visualization by feeling that I was merging my body and mind into an endless blue sky that went on forever.

After a few minutes had passed, I began to feel that the blue sky and I were merging and that I was actually becoming one with the blue sky that stretched on endlessly, in every direction, never beginning and never ending, into infinity.

I continued to hold the image of myself as an infinite blue sky that was both peaceful and blissful, just as *The Handbook* had instructed. I managed to do this fairly effortlessly. My thoughts slowed down much more quickly and without the usual effort it took me, and then without a major act of will on my part, they finally stopped completely.

Unexpected things then started to happen. I was minding my own business being a thoughtless, infinite blue sky of peace and bliss, when Master Fwap and the Oracle suddenly showed up in the middle of my sky!

To make matters even weirder, they were both on snowboards, and Master Fwap had an extra snowboard with him: I recognized it immediately—it was my long board.

The scene changed and I wasn't the sky anymore. I was back in my body, somehow suspended in the sky along with Master Fwap and the Oracle. Looking down, I saw that my long board had attached itself to my feet, although I was standing on my board barefoot like a surfer and didn't have my snowboarding boots on.

Then the world went crazy. Master Fwap and the Oracle began to giggle and, effortlessly turning their snowboards around in the middle of the blue sky, they started to snowboard directly ahead of me on out into the infinite blue sky that lay before us. I figured what the hell and immediately started to skyboard after them.

Without knowing how I could do it, I found that I was able to skyboard through the sky as proficiently as I could snowboard down a mountain on deep powder. The blue sky that the three of us were now skyboarding through had some type of density to it; I was able to cut and carve, as were Master Fwap and the Oracle, against the sky's textured surface. The three of us were truly riding high!

As we skyboarded, we went lower into the blueness, and I could see something up ahead of us that looked like a long red fog bank. When we got very close to it, I could see that it wasn't actually a red fog bank that I was seeing. The sky up ahead was instead composed of lots of different textured layers, all of which were colored in varying hues of red.

Master Fwap unexpectedly cut left, as did the Oracle, and I automatically followed. Master Fwap entered a section of the sky that was composed of a particularly neon pink red, and then suddenly he disappeared. Then the Oracle disappeared into the textured neon pink sky, and I was suddenly alone on my board in the middle of the blue sky.

I aimed my snowboard for the place where I had seen them disappear. When I reached it I heard a loud cracking sound, like thunder, and suddenly I could see them both again boarding on ahead of me. We had entered into a neon red–textured dimension, and we were shooting through it at an incredible speed!

As the three of us boarded the dimension together, I became aware that we were passing over something big. Looking down I saw what I can only describe as a high-tech city passing underneath us. Its buildings were primarily pyramid shaped, and I could see crowds of some sort of beings that looked a little bit like people walking along the streets between the buildings.

But before I could get a further look, I saw a dark violet patch of sky looming ahead of us. Master Fwap aimed for it and disappeared into it. The Oracle and I followed him in.

The violet dimension was charged with more energy than the neon pink dimension had been. I heard a series of loud static explosions similar to the noise a radio makes when a lightning storm causes its speaker to crackle and pop.

The air in this dimension was textured with what looked like some kind of undecipherable hieroglyphic writing. Beings that looked like huge American Indians began flying past us in the air. The giant Indian beings didn't seem to be aware of the three of us. It was like watching TV; I had the sense that I could see them, but they couldn't see us.

Over the course of what seemed like several eternities, Master Fwap, the Oracle, and I skyboarded through hundreds more dimensions. Each dimension we skyboarded through was totally different; some dimensions had beings in them, and some didn't. Each dimension had its own unique color and texture. Some of the dimensions were what I can only describe as "feeling" dimensions, and others were "knowing" dimensions.

The "feeling" dimensions were very emotional for me. Some of them felt very familiar, like I had been in them before. One or two of them produced an intense poignant longing on my part, and I almost didn't want to leave them. There was no pain in any of them; they were all happy places and I wanted to abide in them forever.

But then they would disappear, and we would skyboard into "knowing" dimensions.

I call them "knowing" dimensions because I knew so many different things in each one of them. Memories and prior knowledge would awaken somewhere deep inside of me as we boarded through them. In each of the "knowing" dimensions, I felt like I was a completely different type of person, with a different personality, different memories, and also a different structural knowledge of how the dimension that I was currently skyboarding through worked.

When I would leave one of these "knowing" dimensions, the knowledge, memories, and personality I had briefly assumed would quickly disappear.

During the middle of our interdimensional skyboarding, I opened my eyes. Much to my surprise, I discovered that I was back in the cave of enlightenment. The fire in front of me had almost gone out. I looked at Master Fwap and the Oracle, and as I did, they both opened their eyes and stared back at me. Then the two of them began to laugh.

"What you have just experienced," the Oracle said to me, "was snowboarding through different dimensions. Fwap and I thought that it was time that we introduced you to the high-performance world of astral athletics. How did you like it?"

"I don't know what to say. There was just so much . . . and in some of the dimensions we skyboarded through, I didn't want to come back to this world."

"But you never left it," commented Master Fwap, in a dry tone of voice.

"I mean, sure, if you say so, you know more about this stuff than I do. But I definitely was in a lot of other places at the same time that I was here in this cave."

Both of them laughed heartily, as if I had made some kind of particularly funny joke.

"Master Fwap," I inquired, after their laughter had subsided, "why were you yelling "Phat!" before all of this happened? Is it a word, does it have a special meaning?"

"Yes," he replied. "It is a very powerful mantra. It is normally used to remove impure spirits and forces from a physical area that is connected to interdimensional openings."

"So you two were doing some kind of astral housecleaning when you were engaging in all of that yelling?"

"Yes," he slowly replied. "I have never quite thought about it in that exact way, but I suppose yours is as good a description of what we were doing as any other would be."

"What would your Tantric Buddhist description of it be?" I asked.

"We refer to the mantra as a purification ritual. It is inevitable, just as dust collects in a room over a period of time, that astral forces collect in an interdimensional access area. Most of them are unimportant, but when the location is an interdimensional place of power that is particularly intense—as is the case with the cave we are currently occupying—occasionally powerful negative forces and beings are drawn here. They like the energy that emanates from the cave. But they are destructive forces, and so we must sweep them out.

" 'Phat!' is a particularly powerful mantra that causes them, when it is uttered loudly by a person with occult power, to flee. The vibrational sound of the mantra terrifies these malefic beings, just as dogs are frightened by thunder or the sounds of cannons or guns.

"We have not been to this cave for some years, and it needed a good cleaning," he continued to explain. "Neither the Oracle nor I

181

wanted any of those forces around when we opened the dimensions for you. Some of them might have tried to slip into those beautiful worlds we passed through and tried to bring harm to them."

"How could they do that?"

"On their own, they couldn't. They don't have enough energy to open up the gateways to the higher astral worlds. But if they had slipped in through the gateway, using our power to give them access, they could have polluted or destroyed some of those dimensions and hurt or destroyed some of the higher astral beings that live in them.

"Always use 'Phat!' when you find yourself in an impure or aurically negative physical location, when you need to purify it. Just as fire can purify physical things, the mantra 'Phat!' can purify astral spaces."

I was about to ask Master Fwap the first of several hundred questions that were now exploding into my mind, when he said, "Now we must sleep. We need rest after all of the physical and interdimensional traveling we have done together today. We can talk more about the experience we had this evening tomorrow, if you like."

Master Fwap put more wood on the fire, which had burned down to just a few glowing embers by this time. After he had added the new wood, the fire immediately started to burn and crackle and warm us.

The Oracle retrieved blankets and pads from the back of the cave, and the three of us bedded down in front of the fire. I closed my eyes, then opened them and gazed into the heart of the fire. That was the last thing I remember before falling asleep: the bright red and white flames in the fire pit, burning on into the Himalayan night.

15

THE SNOWBOARDER'S MANTRA

When I awoke the next morning in the cave of enlightenment and rubbed the sleep out of my eyes, I noticed three things: The fire had gone out and I was freezing cold; Master Fwap and the Oracle were nowhere to be seen; and I was still extremely tired from my four days of trekking through the Anapurna Himalayas and probably from my interdimensional skyboarding excursion that had taken place the night before.

I got up, slowly dressed, and lit a fire. I had no idea where the Oracle and Master Fwap had gone. I made myself some tea, and after drinking it, I started to feel a little bit better. My task then was to decide on my next course of action: I could either hang around the cave waiting for Master Fwap and the Oracle to return, or I could leave the cave and go looking for them.

I opted for a middle path instead. Since I was still pretty tired, I thought I would kick back and read from *The Handbook for Enlightenment* for a while, and if they still hadn't returned by the time I had finished my reading, I was going to go snowboarding.

I searched around in my knapsack until I found *The Handbook*. I thumbed through its pages, randomly looking at various chapter titles, searching for something that I might find interesting. After a few minutes I found a section titled "The Ordinary and the Extraordinary Methods." That sounded intriguing.

O nobly born, listen well. There are two correct types of methods and means for the attainment of the all-blissful state of enlightenment: the ordinary and the extraordinary methods.

The ordinary methods are those revealed by enlightened masters in their preliminary instructions. In the case of Lord Buddha, these were the sutras. The sutras outline correct meditation, attitude, intent, mindfulness, and a general introduction to the basics of Buddhist cosmology.

The ordinary methods also include Buddha's second cycle of teachings: the later sutras and the early tantras. Here more advanced methods of meditation, attitude, mindfulness, and an intermediate explanation of Buddhist cosmology are provided. There is some overlap between some of the teachings in Buddha's second cycle of the sutras and the extremely advanced teachings in his third and final cycle of Tantric teachings.

While scholars and pundits may argue as to whether his second cycle of teachings were sutras or tantras, this is not our concern, for we are not interested in what the teachings are called, as revealed by Lord Buddha, Lord Milarapa, Guru Rimpoche, Padma Sambava, Atisha, Lord Krishna, Bodhi Dharma, Lao Tzu, Tilopa, Naropa, or lesser-known enlightened ones.

Nor is our goal to place in competition with each other the systems of Mahayana, Hinayana, Zen, Vadrayana, or other forms of Buddhist, Hindu, or Taoist yoga and Buddhism.

The point of the practice, as outlined in this book, is twofold: (1) after grasping and training oneself in the preliminary methods, to attain the transference of consciousness, which concludes with the great awakening to the clear light of reality, the Dharma kaya—complete enlightenment—the realization of the one without a second; (2) the training to become a Mahasiddha, with the realization that this training—while essentially void in nature, as all training and attainments truly are—allows the practitioner to avoid the trap of limiting the experience of the clear light of reality to the supraconscious realms.

It is only the Mahasiddha who is a pure living mandala, embodying the realization by his existence in all of the worlds that samsara is nirvana.

As Saraha has correctly expressed: "Those fortunate ones who attain the knowledge that from the beginning of endless time mind has never existed realize the mind of the Buddhas of the three eras.

THE EIGHTY-FOUR MAHASIDDHAS

Since the ordinary means of the Buddha's first two cycles of teaching have already been expounded upon in the previous chapters of this handbook and in countless other commentaries and texts, it is the particular point of the last third of *The Handbook for Enlightenment* to transmit to you the extraordinary means by which the eighty-four recognized Mahasid-dhas attained enlightenment.

Know that it was through a blending of both the ordinary means of attainment, which have been previously expounded upon both in this text and in other works, and through the extraordinary means, which follow this introduction, that the Mahasiddhas transformed their impurities into perfections and went beyond the limitations of their perfections to full realization of the inherent emptiness and enlightenment of all.

The eighty-four Mahasiddhas should be seen as mandalas. They provide eighty-four different pathways to enlightenment. You may choose to study one of them and the methods for attainment, several of them, or all eighty-four of them.

The knowledge of more is not necessarily better than the knowledge of a few or even of one of them. It is a matter of individual preference. Our concern here is not the quantity of techniques that you come to know, but that you attain the skillful means by which your enlightenment will blossom.

Therefore, our approach will not be to look at the eighty-four Mahasiddhas individually. Elsewhere in Tantric Buddhist texts their lives and songs have been amply recorded. While it is recommended that you have a general knowledge of all eighty-four of their lives, methods, and songs, what is most important is that you then choose one of the eighty-four, whom you find most appealing or whose circumstances before their realization most resemble your current situation in life, and make that particular Mahasiddha your Tantric root guru and the focus of your study and practice.

Naturally, if you have the priceless opportunity of now studying with a fully enlightened Tantric root guru who is still embodied, his or her instructions will supersede these words. But the best remedy for the illness of illusion is to employ two medicines: the medicine of your current enlightened teacher's knowledge and also the methods revealed in this book that have been used with great success by past enlightened beings, with a particular focus on the eighty-four Mahasiddhas.

If your karma has not led you to an encounter with a fully awakened one in your current lifetime, then use this guide, coupled with the understandings of past cycle awakened ones and the eighty-four Mahasiddhas. Make sure to choose one of the eighty-four Mahasiddhas to be your personal mandala: synchronize your vibration with his aura by repeated study of his life and songs. Meditate upon him, and he will aid you from the other dimensions in your attainment of the emptiness of enlightenment. May your path be filled with joy!

THE SYNTHESES OF THE EIGHTY-FOUR MAHASIDDHAS' TEACHINGS

It is apparent that the eighty-four mahasiddhas all had one thing in common: They practiced the advanced third cycle teachings of Lord Buddha, in which extremely unfortunate circumstances that an individual finds himself in and that would normally make enlightenment impossible are completely reversed into a state of total enlightenment.

These are the extraordinary means and methods: To take what on the surface appear to be impossible circumstances and events that would ordinarily prevent an incarnate being from any attainment whatsoever, and turn those events and circumstances into the springboard to enlightenment.

All eighty-four of the mahasiddhas distinguished themselves through the use of their siddhas as visible proof that they were embodiments of enlightened consciousness. In each of their cases their lives were filled with myriad misfortunes that should have made the attainment of enlightenment impossible. Their attainment proved that Buddha's third cycle of Tantric teachings and methods clearly works. They are intended for use only when the ordinary practices are not sufficient to create enlightenment in one's current life circumstances, and they should be employed only after you have fully mastered the ordinary methods that are revealed in the sutras of Buddha's first and second cycle teachings.

All eighty-four of these great masters of the Vadrayana did not follow the usual monastic methods of practice as elaborated upon in the sutras. While they came from different ranks and castes of society, while they were both women and men, while some were rich and some poor, some educated and some ignorant of reading and writing, all shared one thing in common, which is the essence of all Tantric practice: They were able to turn, in each of their cases, a devastating crisis in their lives into the very means by which they attained the knowledge of the great symbol of total liberation from all limited states of mind.

Intensive study and practice of the advanced tantras will provide you with the means of taking all of the situations that you now see as blocking your practice and turn them into the actual stepping-stones by which you will attain the great realization of nirvana. In short, the inestimable worth and also the proof of the effectiveness of the Tantric teachings is that they can turn lead into gold. When properly understood and practiced, they can help you utilize any real-life situation, no matter how difficult, for proper attainment of enlightenment.

One might say that the tantras show you how to make each seemingly impossible situation in your day-to-day life a monastery in which you can attain total liberation. How wonderful! All earthly experiences can lead to enlightenment when properly employed. This is the essence of the Tantric practices. As Padma Sambava declared upon being exiled from Tibet: "The entire world has now become my monastery."

So, in conclusion, study the following extraordinary methods of the tantras with great diligence. They will provide the skillful means by which you can transform even the most mundane events in your daily life into the pathway to enlightenment. And even in ultimate crisis, their worth—and the worth of Lord Buddha's final cycle of teachings—is therefore proved beyond doubt.

In times when many would say that the attainment of enlightenment was impossible because of circum-

At this point I was maxed out on Buddhist wisdom. I carefully
placed the book back into my knapsack, stood up, and stretched.
Neither Master Fwap nor the Oracle had returned to the cave, so
I decided that it was time to go snowboarding.

After leaving the cave of enlightenment with my snowboarding gear
strapped on my back, I found the narrow path that Master Fwap
had led us down the previous evening and followed it back up to
the main trail. From there I re-ascended the pass, and then I started
to climb up a peak.

It took me about two hours to get to the top. When I got
there I was breathless, covered with sweat, and very happy to have
made it. I guesstimated that I was at around eighteen thousand feet.

Looking down I could see that this run was definitely going
to be the most extreme vertical snowboarding I had ever attempted.
But I was so pumped up from skysurfing the dimensions with Master Fwap and the Oracle that I had a feeling of invulnerability, at
least at first.

After changing my boots, I decided to check out my bindings.
I make it a rule of thumb whenever I do backcountry boarding
always to carry wax, a screwdriver, a stone, ticket wickets, a flash-
light, a lighter, and a simple first-aid kit.

Using my screwdriver I tightened the screws on my bindings. Then I used a little hill wax on some dry spots on my board. I employed the ticket wickets to knock out some little chunks of ice that had collected on my board, and ignored the stone, hoping I would be able to keep on doing so. My stone was only for emergency cut downs, if I shredded my board on some rocks going down and had to shave some slivers off of it.

When I was confident that my gear was in order, I then checked out my mental state. As I have learned through experience, success in extreme snowboarding, as in most other high-performance athletic sports, is more dependent on your state of mind than anything else. Naturally, it is a given that once you are into high-performance sports you will always keep your body in top shape and will constantly practice and improve your technique.

Your mind is a different matter. That is why most snowboarders eventually level out in their evolution in the sport. At a certain point in your snowboarding career, once you have mastered all of the basic, intermediate, and advanced methods, except for the latest trick riding techniques there is really nothing new to learn.

This is the time when most people who have been heavily involved in the sport start to get bored or frustrated with snowboarding. I have never had this problem.

For me, snowboarding, after I had gotten the hang of the physical techniques, became a journey inside of my mind. I discovered that at a certain point in my snowboarding career, further advancement depended on constant practice, mental discipline, and creativity.

I suppose that is why Master Fwap's ideas about Buddhism initially appealed to me, and still do. His view was that your mind's advancement is ultimately the determining factor in your success, once you know what you are doing.

I have talked with a lot of other high-performance athletes

about this, both snowboarders and individuals from other athletic disciplines, including martial artists, scuba divers, mountain climbers, triathletes, surfers, and body builders. All of the pros I have encountered in my athletic travels have agreed: You can take your body only so far; advancement beyond that point is a mental thing.

I don't judge a snowboarder by his jumps or tricks; I watch how he carves and cuts. Too many snowboarders these days are in a rush to get into a photograph or contest. They work on what looks good, not what feels good. In the interest of becoming famous and getting sponsored they neglect to learn how to do a perfect turn, and instead they overfocus on trick riding and jumps.

The fundamental things in snowboarding are your turns and your attitude. You need good gear, technique, and training, as well as common and uncommon sense to survive in backcountry powder. Throw in a good sense of humor for all of the days it doesn't go your way, and you will love the sport as much as I do. But if you really want to excel in snowboarding, or in any high-rev form of athletics, the shape of your mind is ultimately going to be the determining factor.

I snapped my snowboarding boots into their bindings. The clicks sounded solid and right. I shouldered my knapsack and prepared myself for what I anticipated to be the greatest ride of my life. And then, quite unexpectedly, I was filled with fear and dread.

Images of my mangled body, freezing to death on a remote Himalayan peak, began to fill my mind. "Maybe I'm not ready for this yet," I began to think.

Another deeper voice inside of me told me that I was. It wasn't so much a voice as a strong intuitive feeling. I just "knew" I could pull it off—if I could just get my fear under control.

So I began to use the snowboarder's mantra: "No guts, no glory." I just kept repeating it over and over in my mind, until my fear gradually dissipated and then finally stopped. Then I knew I was ready.

I pushed off and started down. I started to cut rhythmically, keeping my mind totally focused on each cut. I didn't allow myself to think of what lay ahead of me or to ego out on a good cut that I had just made. I brought the full power of my mind to bear on each movement I made.

After a few minutes the vertical incline started to ease back, and I switched from cutting on the powder to carving in and out of it. As the slope broadened and the vertical drop evened off into regular off-piste mountain boarding, I started to carve in long, lazy turns. Before I knew it I was at the bottom of the mountain—alive!

I felt an exhilaration that I hadn't felt since I had first started snowboarding. I had just managed to board a mountain that I didn't think I could, and I had done it fairly well. I got off of my board, changed my boots, shouldered my gear, and started looking for the trail that would lead me back to the cave of enlightenment.

I hoped that Master Fwap and the Oracle wouldn't be too pissed off that I had snuck off to go snowboarding. Since I wasn't as telepathic as they were, I knew I wouldn't find out exactly how they felt until I met them back at the cave.

WHY THE BUDDHA LAUGHS LAST

I got back to the cave just before sunset and found Master Fwap and the Oracle busily preparing dinner over the fire pit. I unstrapped my gear, and as the smell of whatever they were cooking hit my nostrils, my mouth began to water, and the hunger in the pit of my stomach instantly awakened.

Psychically sensing my need for carbohydrates, Master Fwap heaped mountains of cooked grains onto my plate. I washed the hot food down with tea, and then, overcome with a complete sense of well-being, I sat back by the warmth of the fire with a full stomach and with my greatest athletic achievement still fresh in my memory. Then I lay down on my sleeping pad and stared at the flickering shadows cast by the fire as they danced across the top of the cave.

"Did your snowboarding go well?" Master Fwap politely inquired.

"Yes," I responded in a mellow voice. "I think that today I reached a new level in my snowboarding capabilities."

"Don't you think that your snowboard, this cave, this place of power, Fwap and I, and your experience last night in the second attention surfing the dimensions also deserve part of the credit for your 'success' today?" the Oracle asked me in a humorous tone of voice. "Fwap, it sounds to me like our young friend's ego is beginning to blossom nicely," he added, with a sarcastic grin.

"Now, now, O great Oracle of Nepal," Master Fwap immediately responded. "Don't you think we should perhaps take it easy on the boy? Tomorrow he must see if he can overcome the initial 'obstacle,' to see if his power is strong enough to attempt to solve the riddle of the missing dimensions. I am not sure that criticizing him now will help him to overcome the obstacle, but as always, O great and powerful Oracle of Nepal, I bow to your superior wisdom in these matters."

"Wait a minute, you guys," I said, interrupting their conversation. "What do you mean that I have to overcome an obstacle tomorrow before I get to tackle the riddle? We just got here," I said nervously.

"Tomorrow is your day," responded the Oracle. "Don't worry, I think the whole obstacle challenge is a waste of your time. You should solve the riddle right away, and then begin your study of the third cycle of the Buddha's Tantric teachings, so that you can regain your past-life enlightenment as soon as possible. But Fwap is insistent on following all of the proper etiquette and formalities. That's because he's older than I am and still stuck in some of the old-school Buddhist ways. I think that the obstacle is a waste of your time and energy. We should get on with solving the riddle and teaching you what you need to know now, before you return to the West."

"Wait a minute. You said that once I solved the riddle that would be it; I would know everything that I needed to know in order to become enlightened. You never mentioned anything about overcoming an obstacle before I dealt with the riddle!" I interjected in a frustrated tone of voice.

"And what about the disembodied master who spoke to me

out on the peak? He too seemed to think that I had to solve the riddle pronto, I mean, he seemed very concerned about the fact that the dimensions were disappearing. Master Fwap told me he was posing a riddle for me to solve that would help me—if I succeeded in solving it—to become enlightened.

"The two of you confirmed this, and we trekked all of the way out here to do it. What gives? Is this one of your Buddhist jokes?"

"Not at all," Master Fwap responded. "The obstacle is real, and solving it will help you the day after tomorrow, when you attempt to solve the riddle of the missing dimensions. If you succeed in overcoming the obstacle tomorrow, and in solving the riddle the day after tomorrow, you will still need both the Oracle's and my empowerments and explanations to move from a conceptual understanding of the more advanced Tantric methods and practices to the actual knowledge and experience of them."

"Let me see if I am getting this straight. Even if I overcome the obstacle—whatever that might be—and then successfully solve the riddle, you two expect me to stay here in Nepal even longer and study the advanced Tantric stuff with you?"

"Definitely," Master Fwap replied. "I am afraid there is no other way in this age to find out what you must know."

"Most definitely!" shouted the Oracle. "You're not going to escape from your karma so easily. Don't feel bad, though. Both Fwap and I have gone through the same mental states you are currently experiencing, and we have an understanding of your frustrations."

"Hold on a minute here, you two. I came to Nepal to snowboard the Himalayas. I ran into Master Fwap, and he told me that studying Buddhism would make me a better snowboarder. He performed miracles in front of my eyes and transported me into levels of perfect awareness and knowledge that I didn't even know existed. Then I came here, to this cave, with the both of you, to improve my snowboarding through learning more about Buddhism.

"Now this whole thing is beginning to sound more like going to college," I complained. "Once I pass one course, I just get stuck in the next, more advanced course. I know for sure that I am not ready for college yet, as a matter of fact, I don't know if I ever will be."

"Do you know why the Buddha always laughs last?" Master Fwap asked me.

"You know that I don't know why the Buddha always laughs last. What does that have to do with what we were just discussing?"

"Everything and nothing," responded the Oracle.

"Okay, why does the Buddha always laugh last?" I inquired, my frustration growing with each passing moment.

"He laughs last because he didn't laugh first," Master Fwap responded, in a serious tone of voice.

"What is that supposed to mean, and what does that have to do with overcoming the obstacle and finding the secret of the missing dimensions, and then with my having to stay here longer in Nepal and study the advanced tantras with the both of you?"

"It's the easiest way to overcome the obstacle," the Oracle commented with a yawn.

"But what does it all mean? Obstacle? Missing dimensions? Advanced tantras?" I asked.

"Nothing at all," responded Master Fwap.

"Well, if you'll excuse me, that sounds pretty dumb. What's the point of a question that has an answer that doesn't mean anything at all?"

"I told you the obstacle was a waste of time," the Oracle said with a bored expression on his face. "But Fwap is definitely a man who believes in the old ways, so I suppose we must go through this."

"Indeed, we must!" Master Fwap replied with renewed vigor in his voice.

"Okay, I'll listen. But I want you both to know, no disrespect intended, that I am definitely in my heavy skepticism mode," I said as a tone of righteous indignation began to creep into my voice.

"So what else is new?" inquired the Oracle.

"The obstacle is why the Buddha laughs last. His laughing last is not the obstacle. This is a clue that should enable you, after you understand the half-life of time, to overcome the obstacle with ease," Master Fwap said in a formal tone.

"Once you have overcome the obstacle and solved the riddle, we will lead you through the advanced tantras. All of this I promise you will further improve your snowboarding and also provide you with the skillful means to do something much more important, namely, to become enlightened."

"I feel like you two are setting me up here."

"We are," responded Master Fwap.

"We are," echoed the Oracle.

"But we are not setting you up for something unhappy or unfortunate," Master Fwap continued. "Remember, our Buddhist humor is based on making others happy. We take no joy in the difficulties, misfortunes, or frustrations of others.

"Yes, indeed, we are setting you up. We are setting you up to be the best snowboarder you can be and to regain your past-life enlightenment. We are setting you up for very happy things. But it is necessary to coerce your mind just a little bit to get you to go along with us. Trust us. Later you will be very glad that you did."

"Should we tell him about the German woman who snowboards better than he does?" the Oracle asked Master Fwap with a huge grin on his face.

"What German woman? I didn't know there were any women who could snowboard better than I can!"

"Well, I suppose we might make a casual mention of it to him, O great Oracle of Nepal, now that you have let the proverbial cat out of the bag."

"Tell me about her, Master Fwap. Please!"

"All right, but don't get too excited or it will distract you from overcoming the obstacle tomorrow. If you don't overcome the obstacle and then solve the riddle, you will never get to meet her.

"It's really quite simple," Master Fwap continued. "A young woman arrived in Nepal from Germany to snowboard the Himalayas. But she is just a little bit better at snowboarding than you are."

"Is she another Buddhist like Nadia was?" I hesitantly asked.

"No, as a matter of fact, she has absolutely no interest in metaphysics. She is a student in Heidelberg, studying philosophy. She is very pragmatic and doesn't believe in anything to do with the spirit. She is definitely physically based," Master Fwap said in summation.

"There is one hitch, though," the Oracle said, trying unsuccessfully to suppress a grin.

"What's that?" I asked suspiciously.

"Should I tell him, Fwap?"

"It won't hurt at this point."

"What's the hitch, Master Oracle?" I asked as my curiosity became aroused.

"Nothing very big. You've just been with her in about a dozen of your past lives, that's all."

I was struck dumb for several minutes, absorbing everything that Master Fwap and the Oracle had just told me.

The Oracle then broke the silence: "Well, don't you want to know why the Buddha always laughs last?" he asked with a twinkle in his eyes.

"Yes," I immediately responded. "Why, Master Oracle?"

The Oracle was silent for a moment. He closed his eyes briefly, and then reopened them and stared directly at me. "The reason that the Buddha always laughs last is because he sees the ephemeral nature of existence. In the world of Buddhist enlightenment there is always laughter and never tragedy.

"Things may appear tragic on the surface, but all of the so-called tragedies of life eventually melt away in the white light of time. Without time and death, there can be no permanent tragedy or separation. In each of our incarnations we are drawn back to what we love, and those we love, and the so-called tragedies that we experienced in our previous lifetime only become our next in-carnation's past-life memories.

"Since the Buddha, and all enlightened beings for that matter, know this, they always have the last laugh. It is not an egotistical laugh," he continued. "It's a happy laugh at the delightful play of existence, which only enlightened masters can accurately see from their cosmic perspectives.

"Now that you understand this, all that is left to prepare you to overcome the obstacle and to solve the riddle of the missing dimensions is a proper understanding of the half-life of time. Fwap will guide you through those mysteries, while I sit here and tend to the fire."

17

THE HALF-LIFE OF TIME

"I am definitely confused about the secret of the missing dimensions, Master Fwap. You say that it is important for me to solve it because my future enlightenment depends on it. Now you have added that I must overcome the obstacle before I can solve the riddle.

"The Oracle tells me that it doesn't matter if I overcome the obstacle or not. And now you're telling me about another woman I am going to meet in Katmandu, whom I have know in many of my past lives, who you claim is a better snowboarder than I am. Right now I think I am a victim of information overload. Can you help me sort all of this out, please?" I begged him in a stressed-out and plaintive voice.

"Certainly. The Oracle is only playing a joke on you. He knows as well as I do the importance of overcoming the obstacle first. As far as the young German snowboarder we alluded to, it is true you have been close with her in other lifetimes. She has, at least at this point in her incarnation, no knowledge of her spiritual potential at all. She does not recall ever being with you or practicing yoga in her past lives, either. As a matter of fact, at the moment, she thinks that the whole concept of Tantric Buddhist yoga and magic is based on the superstitions of an ignorant third world culture.

"If you overcome the obstacle tomorrow, and solve the riddle the day after tomorrow, it will then be your karma to encounter her in Katmandu and go snowboarding with her. What will come of this, I am not sure.

"Once you have overcome the obstacle, solved the riddle, completed your karma with your past-life German snowboarding friend, and finished your studies of the advanced tantras with the Oracle and me, you will have all the resources at your command to return to America and become enlightened.

"As I have told you before, upon your return to America you must go back to college, get a Ph.D., continue practicing the Tantric methods, regain your past-life enlightenment, and also become wealthy and famous. Only then will some of the people in your culture bother to listen to what you have to say about enlightenment.

"One day, you will write a series of books about your experiences with me and the Oracle. They will be translated into many languages and bring comfort and understanding to millions of people.

"It is also your karma to become involved with transmitting the higher energy of enlightened consciousness through music, something we have been doing in the East for thousands of years. Your music will be Western, even though it carries the energy of Eastern happiness and enlightenment with it. This will not be as difficult for you as you might suppose, since you have been a composer in several of your past incarnations.

"Also, you will enter into the world of computers and computer software. Computers hold the future for this planet. Your innate mathematical and design skills, which you also acquired in previous incarnations, will make you very successful in that field.

"Everything will not be perfect for you. There will also be

great pain in your life. Once you have returned to the West, when you attempt to share your knowledge of the Tantric enlightenment methods and practices, most of the people there will think that you are a charlatan.

"Even if they believed that a person from the West could become enlightened to begin with—which most of them don't— they wouldn't believe that you were for real. In addition, since your enlightenment would be actual and not intellectual, you wouldn't be telling them what they want to hear. You will tell them the truth.

"The truth has never been particularly popular either here in the East or in your Western world. Since you most certainly will want to transmit the experience of enlightenment and not be content simply to provide the intellectual understanding of enlightenment that people really want, you will be reviled.

"Almost no one will believe what you have to say, and you will be a stranger in your own land. What a thought!" Master Fwap said with a laugh. "A Caucasian attempting to teach the eternal truths of Buddhist enlightenment in a Western way in a Western world! No one will understand you or what you say because you will not fit into the pre-formatted ideas that Westerners have about how enlightened people should look, act, live, and speak!

"As I have told you before, it is not so different here in the East even for me and the Oracle. Real masters don't act the way that people expect them to. False masters do.

"If and when you overcome the obstacle and solve the riddle, you have a life of hard work and social enmity ahead of you. This will be more than counterbalanced for you, however, by the joy and ecstasy that living in enlightened states of mind will bring. Your outer life may be filled with unfortunate circumstances, but your inner life will be perfect.

"If you choose not to overcome the obstacle and solve the riddle, then none of this will happen. You can merrily go ahead snowboarding your way through life and not have to go through all of the pains and responsibilities that would otherwise await you. There are good reasons to overcome the obstacle and solve the riddle and good reasons not to."

"But, Master Fwap!" I protested. "You told me that you wouldn't tell me, out of Buddhist courtesy, whether I had really solved the riddle or not. How will I know if I have really done it or if I am just kidding myself?"

"In your case, the Oracle and I have seen in our meditation that we need to make an exception. You will not have to wait many years to know whether you have solved the riddle, although it will take you many years to unravel its meaning and to be able to benefit fully from its meaning, if you do succeed."

"But how will I know?"

"If, the day after tomorrow, we invite you back to Katmandu to teach you more about the advanced tantras, then you will know that you have overcome the obstacle and solved the riddle of the missing dimensions. Also, if you have solved the riddle successfully, you will meet your new German snowboarding companion. The Oracle and I will then take you both snowboarding on some even more challenging peaks than the ones you have snowboarded down so far. The advanced methods that you will gain from the study of the later tantras will improve your snowboarding skills considerably. You may even learn to snowboard as well as your past-life German snowboarding friend.

"Now, is everything clear to you?" he asked me in a very patient tone of voice.

"Yes, Master Fwap. Thank you for clearing all of this up for me. I guess I just have one question left: What is the half-life of time anyway?"

Master Fwap closed his eyes, as did the Oracle. The two of them began to spontaneously meditate. I decided it would be wise to join them, and so I folded my legs in a cross-legged position, closed my eyes, and started to practice my meditation technique.

My visualization of the "Blue Sky" started as it had the evening before. I followed all of the steps as outlined in *The Handbook for Enlightenment*. My thoughts began to slow down, and finally they stopped completely.

Throughout my meditation, some distant part of me kept expecting Master Fwap and the Oracle to show up in the middle of my blue sky, so that we could continue our adventures in surfing the dimensions, but they never came. Instead, I simply had a beautiful meditation in which I felt great peace and a oneness with all of life.

My meditation was interrupted when I was distracted by a sound. When I opened my eyes, Master Fwap and the Oracle had finished their respective meditations and were bowing and touching their foreheads to the cave floor. I respectfully did the same.

After sitting in silence for several minutes, Master Fwap and the Oracle turned and faced me. Both of their eyes were filled with gentleness and an otherworldly light.

"Now it is time to talk about the half-life of time," Master Fwap began. "Once again, I must caution you not to reason out what I am about to say. For now, just accept it as it is. Let my words flow into your second attention. If you have any questions about my explanation, I am sure they will be better answered by the experiences you will have tomorrow.

"To begin to understand the half-life of time, consider the following. Consciousness in this and most other dimensions exists because of time. Time is the movement of life. In the advanced technological countries of the West, you understand a great deal more about the 'things' of the world than we simple Buddhist peasants do. You understand and take pride in the fact that you can build and fly airplanes, erect giant skyscrapers, probe the solar system with telescopes, and examine cells and viruses with the aid of microscopes. This is the way of the modern world, to 'understand' a great deal about many different types of things.

"The way of the old world—our third world Vadrayana Tantric Buddhist culture—is not to understand very much at all. We don't understand all that you understand about life. Yet even in the midst of our third world economic poverty, we are rich in something that you don't have in the West; we are rich in our 'knowing' of how life and the universe work, and we are happy in our personal experience of our interrelationship with them.

"As I have said to you before, understanding is an intellectual type of knowledge. It is very useful. It can help you to lead a better life by giving you cures for diseases, or it can cause harm when misused by creating and employing weapons for mass destruction.

"Knowing life and oneself, and the subtle interrelationships between both, are far different from the mere dry, conceptual understanding of things. To know something is to become it, to experience it, to revel in it, and to become a part of its essence and power.

"Both knowledge and understanding are important to have. They are like yin and yang, they are complements, not opposites. Without each other they exist in a state of imbalance. Together they create something entirely new when unified—tai chi, the fullness of existence.

206

"The problem that you are having—which is my way of expressing to you the way to move from your current level of intellectual understanding to direct intuitive knowledge—has to do with having a correct 'knowing' of time. If you simply understand time without the 'knowledge' of time, you are existing in a state of imbalance. You are like yin without yang; you are incomplete.

"As with yin and yang, when you put the understanding of time together with the knowledge of time, you are not just adding one and one together and coming up with two. Combining your Western understanding of time with our Eastern knowledge of time will create something totally new for you: It will provide you with a much larger and more expansive view of existence, yourself, and the interrelationship between yourself and the web of life. In other words, the sum of the two when combined will far exceed their 'mass' if you were simply to add them together.

"It is like a man and a woman," he continued. "They are quite different. But when they join in sexual union they create a new life, a baby, which is really like neither of them. True, the baby will have certain genetic traits present in its DNA that came from both of its parents. Yet it will have an independent structure and existence that, in truth, resemble neither of its parents.

"So all you lack to overcome the obstacle tomorrow is the knowledge of the half-life of time." Master Fwap paused for a few minutes and shifted his position on his meditation cushion. He sat up straight as an arrow, closed his eyes, and finished his explanation of the half-life of time with his eyes shut.

"The half-life of time," he said in a quiet tone of voice, which forced me to focus my full attention on every word he said, "is the correct perceptual awareness of the movement of life. From the point of view of the average person, time keeps on slipping into the future, making the past a mere memory. To them it appears that time is the causative agent in the movement of existence. From this point of view, time is the cause of birth, growth, maturation, death, and eventual rebirth. This is the common conceptual understanding of time. It has mass, because mass is required to create energy, which creates the moment of time.

"Now knowing time is very different from understanding time. To know time you must first know life. And the best way to know life is to dance. In most of what you would refer to as 'primitive' cultures, where people know and respect life, its mysteries, themselves, and all other living beings, the people dance together.

"Yes, it is true, you have dancing in your culture, but your dancing is simply a prelude to sexuality, an entirely different type of dance than the dance we have here in the East. The dances of the 'primitive' peoples of the world, all of whom don't 'understand' too much but 'know' a great deal, have two features that you lack in your Western dance. First, the dances here and the dancers of the dance tell stories through their dancing, stories of their individual lives and also of the experiences of their tribes.

"The second difference is that through this type of dance, people are able to lift themselves into higher perceptual states in which they are able to go beyond their intellectual understanding of time and experience the true knowledge of time directly.

"Don't look so puzzled," Master Fwap said with a happy laugh. "You know exactly what I am talking about. Dancing for the 'primitive' people of the world is a form of meditation through which they either individually, or collectively as a group, rise above their intellectual understandings of life and come to know and experience time and life directly.

"You are doing the same thing when you go snowboarding. It is the very reason you snowboard. When you snowboard perfectly your thoughts stop and you rise above time. You enter into a

208

timeless dimension where you experience great joy. When you rise above your ego and its conceptual understandings of life, you experience the pure joy and ecstasy of the web of life.

"The half-life of time is the awareness that time doesn't have either mass or energy. It is like a magician's trick; time appears to have more substance than it really does. Time is insubstantial and ineffable, and to be completely honest with you, it doesn't really even exist at all," Master Fwap continued to explain. "Perhaps this is why Einstein, a man who came from the country that has perfected the measurement of time, was the first Westerner to really come to a partial knowing of the half-life of time, which he expressed in his now famous equation: $E = mc^2$.

"This may seem strange to you, but try to understand that time doesn't change; time is only an idea that human beings have invented for themselves. At best it is merely a convenient conceptual way to measure small segments of eternity.

"Nothing is ever born, nothing grows, nothing matures, and nothing decays or dies, nor is anything really reborn. This is true, because, in reality, there is nothing there to begin with. The perception that existence exists, and that time has mass and reality, and that it changes, are illusions created by a person's concept of self. The self itself is an illusion.

"Show me yourself!" Master Fwap challenged me. "Not your physical body, your real self! You cannot: Your self, like time, is only an idea. In deep meditation, when your thoughts are stopped, the awareness of your illusory self ceases. This is true knowledge. As you yourself have experienced in altered states of consciousness, there is no sense of time or self as there is in this world, because, in reality, there is really no time."

"But, Master Fwap, in other dimensions I have experienced time and self; they were just different types of time and self."

"That is exactly what I mean by the knowledge of time and self. What you come to understand is that there is not just one type of time and self. There are an infinite number of times and selves—and there is something more. Beyond all of the times and selves of the universe there is nirvana. Nirvana is timeless and self-less. That is why it cannot be discussed or even experienced, since you need a self to do that. Since time and self don't exist in nirvana, nirvana can only be 'known.'"

"But if nirvana can only be known, there must be some type of self that is experiencing that knowing," I countered.

"No, not really," Master Fwap replied. "This is all just a way of talking about something that cannot be talked about. You will know this only when you come to 'know' nirvana; it is a knowledge that passes beyond understanding, beyond both the knower and what is known.

"It is your illusory self that creates the illusion that you are passing through time and space, neither of which, in reality, exists. In truth there is only emptiness. The world, its myriad beings, dimensions, and times, is like a dream. When you are experiencing a dream, it seems very real. But upon awakening, you realize that what seemed real and substantial while your were dreaming actually had no substance at all. Your dream disappears upon waking.

"Enlightenment is the waking from the dream of life. When you become enlightened, you awaken to emptiness. Emptiness implies absence. Not the absence of reality, but the absence of illusions.

"When you are enlightened, you awaken from the half-life of time and self. What you awaken to, and who you awaken as, cannot be understood here. That can only be known, in the true sense in which I use the word 'knowing,' when you are in a state of perpetually enlightened consciousness.

"The half-life of time is the half-life you are currently living in your waking dreams, which you refer to as your conscious experiences. From the perspective of the enlightened, you are sleepwalking your way through life. You are surrounded by others who are doing the same, believing that the lives they are dreaming are real and substantial, when in fact they are only ephemeral and transitory dreams.

"Only the enlightened are truly awakened, since they have transcended the half-life of time. Only they can see and know the difference between illusions and truth."

Master Fwap finished, and for once, I had nothing to say. I looked first at him, and then at the Oracle. I knew I didn't completely understand most of what Master Fwap had just explained to me, but at least I was consciously aware of the fact that I didn't really understand: I hoped that some day I might fully know what he was talking about.

The air in the cave grew colder as the late afternoon began to turn into early evening. Master Fwap placed more wood on the fire. My mind was completely silent, and I was pleasantly overwhelmed by a sense of contentment. Staring into the fire, as I watched its flames burn and transform the pieces of wood into ash, heat, smoke, and flames, I knew that the wood wasn't really being destroyed; it just appeared that way through the illusion of the half-life of time. The wood was as it always had been, even though its outer form was now ash and smoke. In reality, it existed as it always had and would, just on the other side of understanding, just past the half-life of time.

I lay down next to the fire and drifted off into a dreamless sleep, which I remained in, until Master Fwap and the Oracle awakened me the next morning.

18

SNOWBOARDING TO NIRVANA

Master Fwap and the Oracle awakened me at dawn.

"Well," said the Oracle with a slight chuckle, "this is your big day. Today you will either overcome the obstacle or you won't."

"What is the obstacle, Master Oracle?" I asked, still rubbing the sleep out of my eyes.

"The obstacle is simple—you have to snowboard to nirvana. Fwap and I will help you. It's similar to what we were doing the other day, when we were surfing the dimensions with you. The only difference is that you must surf beyond the dimensions until you reach what we refer to as the obstacle. If you manage to cross it, then you will reach nirvana, which lies just beyond it. While Fwap and I will help you to get started by opening up the missing dimensions for you so that you can enter into them, we will not be able to join you on your expedition. We will be watching, though."

"Master Oracle," I inquired in a sleepy voice, "if I snowboard successfully to nirvana, does that mean I will have become enlightened?"

"No, I'm afraid not." he said, laughing crazily.

The way he laughed made me feel as if I had just told him a very funny Buddhist joke. I asked him about it. He replied as follows: "Yes, you have just unwittingly told one of the funniest Buddhist jokes I have heard in a long time."

"What was the punch line? I don't get my own joke," I asked, a little embarrassed, and frustrated as well.

"*You* are the punch line!" he said with more laughter, "but don't worry about it now. You won't understand until you become enlightened. And as you know by now, when you become enlightened, you won't understand anything at all!

"But it is all right," he resumed, once he got his laughter under control. "After you become enlightened, you may not understand the joke, but at least you'll 'know' why it is funny. Let's return to your original question. You wanted to know if overcoming the obstacle and reaching nirvana will make you enlightened, is that right?"

"Yes."

"No, you won't become enlightened. But you will have entered into samadhi for the first time. There are three primary types of samadhi: *salvikalpa, nirvakalpa,* and *sahaja,*" he continued to explain to me.

"*Salvikalpa* samadhi is a very advanced meditative state in which you will have a brief glimpse of nirvana; it's an epiphany on a grand scale.

"Later, when you can attain *nirvakalpa* samadhi at will, then you will have become enlightened.

"*Sahaja* samadhi is fully integrated enlightenment. That is the stateless state of enlightenment that Fwap and I exist in. In Sanskrit, we refer to it as the dharma kaya, or freely translated, the 'clear light of reality.'

In *sahaja* samadhi, Fwap and I don't have to close our eyes, as one does in *nirvakalpa* samadhi or *salvikalpa* samadhi, in order to experience nirvana. In *sahaja* samadhi we are always immersed in nirvana, whether our eyes are open or shut, or whether we are awake or asleep.

"No, today you will just have to be satisfied with a brief glimpse of nirvana. You will get this when you overcome the obstacle. Then we will know that your power is keen enough to tackle the secret of the missing dimensions tomorrow."

"So the secret of the missing dimensions is not that they are missing, is that right?"

"Precisely," he replied. "To say that they are missing, as Fwap explained to you before, is just our way of talking about them. They are not really missing, they haven't been lost, misplaced, or stolen. To say that they are missing is our way of explaining why they are so hard to see. As Fwap has told you, there are simply too many people on the earth now, and the combined effects of all of their auras is like an eclipse of the sun.

"During an eclipse, the sun is still there, but the moon comes between the earth and the sun, so the sun can't be seen. The dimensions simply cannot be seen, found, or opened now, because there are vibrating fields of human auras on our planet. We have passed the five billion person mark and are on our way toward ten or fifteen billion.

"The secret of the missing dimensions lies within them. You have to enter them and experience them to learn what their secret is. With our combined power, Fwap and I can still perceive and open the dimensions, something that you would find impossible to do. We can get you in, but once you are there, it is your job on your own, without our help, to solve their riddle.

"Today you will have our help and guidance. The closest I can come to explaining what we will be doing for you today, once you are inside of the dimensions, is that we will be empowering your

214

aura to make your passage to the shores of nirvana possible. On your own, you don't have enough power yet either to find and open the missing dimensions or to attain *salvikalpa* samadhi.

"Remember," the Oracle cautioned me, "I am describing nirvana as if it were a physical location that you have to travel to, and the obstacle as if it were a physical boundary that you have to jump over. In reality, the obstacle and nirvana are both within your own mind. I use physical analogies because I don't have any other way to explain any of this to the logical portion of your mind.

"What you are really aiming your sights on today," he continued, "is spiritual realization, a knowing, an experience, something that cannot be known or explained through words, comparisons, analogies, or similes here in dimensional space. Are you ready to begin?"

"Sure, I guess so," I answered with some slight hesitation and trepidation.

"Good. First we will all drink some tea and you can wash up, then we will begin!"

After washing up with melted snow water, and drinking tea in silence with Master Fwap and the Oracle, I knew the time had come. I could feel the power inside of the cave increasing; it felt like waves of static electricity were passing through the cave of enlightenment and entering into my body; each wave felt stronger than its predecessor.

Master Fwap then spoke to me in his formal Buddhist master's voice: "The three of us will sit in meditation, as we did two days ago. You will use your astral snowboard to surf the dimensions, and if it is your karma, today you will snowboard to nirvana."

215

. . .

The three of us sat together as we had two days before, with the Oracle sitting in a cross-legged position on my right side and Master Fwap sitting on my left. I closed my eyes and started to use the "Blue Sky" meditation technique. After a few minutes, my thoughts began to slow down, and then, quite abruptly, they stopped.

I found myself in the blue astral sky again. Only this time I was on my short snowboard. In the distance ahead of me I saw the red fog bank that I had seen on my last interdimensional skyboarding expedition, and I immediately headed right for it.

Passing into it, I entered the neon red dimension again. I then in rapid succession passed into and through each dimension that Master Fwap, the Oracle, and I had experienced two days before, until I saw something up ahead of me that I hadn't seen before.

What lay ahead of me appeared to be a series of phosphorescent circles. Their circumferences seemed to be continually expanding. I aimed for the center of the first one and was about to enter into it when I was all of a sudden overcome with fear. I suddenly felt frozen with terror, as I had the day before out on the peak.

I was so scared that I stopped my board. I have never been so afraid of anything before or since.

I wanted immediately to board away from the soft white phosphorescent circles of light. It was a totally irrational fear, but it was real for me nevertheless.

Then without knowing how I understood, I simply knew what the obstacle was. It was my own fear of the unknown. Hanging there in interdimensional space, on my astral snowboard, I started mentally to repeat the snowboarder's mantra, "No guts, no glory," over and over again, until my fear started to subside.

After getting my fears under control, I took aim at the phosphorescent circles of light and shot through the first one. Then I went through the second, third, and fourth.

I boarded through hundreds of circles of light until, without knowing how, I lost myself somewhere in the middle of nowhere. I didn't exist anymore.

I had a vague awareness of a kind that I cannot put into words, an awareness of the entire universe. All that I can express in words is that time ceased to exist for me, motion ceased to exist for me, and any awareness of both my individuality or of the rest of the universe as being either separate from myself or a part of myself ceased.

I cannot describe what it was like, because there is nothing that I have ever experienced before in the physical or astral dimensions to compare it to.

I remained as that timeless awareness forever. Changes occurred yet didn't occur; it was like floating in space, except I wasn't there and space wasn't space. There is simply no way to express to you what I experienced as nirvana or to find any analogies to express what it was like.

After experiencing infinity—or whatever it was—without experiencing it, I found myself opening my eyes. Both Master Fwap and the Oracle had their eyes open and were keenly observing me.

I couldn't even talk at first. No thoughts or words would come. I felt like I wanted to say something to them, to thank them for sharing a view of life that was light-years beyond the power of understanding and experience.

Master Fwap and the Oracle just continued looking at me, and without knowing how I knew, I was sure that they understood. The peace in their eyes and the gentle smiles on their faces explained everything.

"I didn't know, Master Fwap and Master Oracle. I have had some beautiful meditations before with you, but this was so far beyond anything ... I don't know what to say. How long have I been meditating?"

"Oh, about four hours," Master Fwap replied.

"Four hours!" I exclaimed. "Master Fwap, it seemed like about forty minutes at most."

"There is no way to explain any of this, nor should you try," counseled the Oracle. "The best thing for us to do right now is to take a hike and go view the beauty of the Anapurnas while it is still daylight. Their beauty will do all of the talking for us."

The three of us rose. I put on my coat, boots, and gloves, and we left the cave. Outside the sunlight reflecting off the Himalayan snow was blindingly bright. I instinctively reached inside of my coat pocket, retrieved and put my on my sunglasses.

We walked for several hours. Then the three of us returned to the cave just before sunset. Standing outside of the cave we watched the most beautiful Himalayan sunset I had ever seen.

It was like a laser light show at a Pink Floyd concert, but better: I saw every possible color in the clouds in the sky filtering down and filling the passes between the Anapurna Himalayas, with a degree of clarity I had never possessed before. It was even better than the "Blue Flash" at Malibu.

After the sun had set we entered the cave. Removing my gear, I sat down in front of the fire that Master Fwap had just started. The Oracle was busily making tea.

"So, you have had your first meditative experience of samadhi," the Oracle remarked. "It was only a slight experience, but it will change your karma forever. You will never again see life in quite the same way as you did before today.

"You are definitely ready now!" he continued with great enthusiasm. "Tomorrow you will try, on your own, to solve the riddle of the missing dimensions. Master Fwap and I will help you enter into those dimensions, but you must, under your own power, solve their riddle and then find your way back out to the 'just right' location.

"That is the riddle," he said, as a large smile broadened across his face. "If you exit the missing dimensions at the karmically correct location, you will have solved the riddle of the missing dimensions!"

After that, the Oracle, Master Fwap, and I had tea and later a hot meal. We spent the remainder of the evening in silence, listening to the Himalayan winds swirling fresh snow around the entrance to the cave of enlightenment.

EPILOGUE

The Secret of the Missing Dimensions

I now knew what the secret of the missing dimensions was! Master Fwap and the Oracle were congratulating me on my having discovered it. Now it was simply a matter of trekking back through the beautiful Anapurna Himalayas, meeting a world-class German snowboarder, and studying the advanced Tantric texts with Master Fwap and the Oracle. "No problemo," I thought to myself. Then I woke up.

I was lying on the cold cave floor. The fire had gone out, and I could vaguely see the interior of the cave as the first light of morning filtered in through the cave's mouth.

My body was covered with several rough woolen blankets; evidently Master Fwap or the Oracle had placed them over me, after I had fallen asleep the evening before.

It was only a dream! I hadn't solved the riddle yet, and I didn't know if I would be able to. "Nice dream," I sarcastically thought to myself. Before I could think any further, Master Fwap and the Oracle came walking into the cave.

"Still sleeping?" inquired the Oracle. "Do all Americans sleep as much as you do?"

I assumed that his question was rhetorical, so I didn't bother to answer it.

"Time to get up and take a crack at the riddle," Master Fwap

220

stated in a matter-of-fact tone of voice. "It is much easier for us to open up the dimensions for you at sunrise, sunset, or late in the evening. Since you are well rested now, and you may be tired by this evening, let's get started. You'll need all of the energy you can possibly muster to solve the riddle and discover the secret of the missing dimensions today."

I got up and stretched. There was no need to get dressed since I had fallen asleep in my clothes. While Master Fwap started a fire and the Oracle began walking around the cave shouting "Phat!" I ducked outside for a few minutes, and after taking care of nature's morning call, I washed my hands and face thoroughly with some of the new powder that had fallen the night before.

The iciness of the snow upon my face awakened me immediately. I returned to the cave and sat down in front of the fire to warm myself. Master Fwap served himself and me some tea, while the Oracle continued to walk around the cave shouting "Phat!"

After a while the Oracle stopped shouting the mantra and joined us. As usual, he sat on my left side while Master Fwap sat on my right. Master Fwap poured and handed the Oracle a cup of tea, which the Oracle proceeded to sip very loudly.

When we had all finished our tea, Master Fwap spoke: "Meditate with us, and the rest will follow."

"That's it, Master Fwap? No other instructions?" I asked with amazement. In the back of my mind, I had assumed that he was going to give me one of his long preliminary talks, as he usually did before he asked me to try a new type of Buddhist practice.

"That is all, just meditate," he said.

"If I were you, I would listen to Fwap," the Oracle remarked offhandedly.

"Okay," I replied. For some reason it seemed to me that there should have been more of a ceremony involved, or that I should have had something eloquent to say to them, but "okay" was all I could come up with at the time.

I closed my eyes and started the "Blue Sky" visualization. After picturing the blue sky for a few minutes, I began to see a lot of different reds, greens, yellows, blues, and a particular shade of turquoise I had never seen before, swirling around me.

Then I saw the white puffy circles of light that I had passed through the day before. But I didn't feel as if I was in my astral body, and I couldn't manage to move toward the circles of light.

They, however, moved toward me. One circle of light after another passed around me. They looked like phosphorescent circles that were made up of light and fluffy cumulus clouds.

I felt timeless again. The circles of light unexpectedly disappeared, and I found myself sitting in what appeared to be Master Fwap's meditation room at his monastery in Katmandu. Master Fwap was sitting on my right, and the Oracle was sitting on my left.

I looked from one to the other. They both had the biggest smiles on their faces that I had ever seen.

"The American boy has done it, Fwap. Phat!" shouted out the Oracle with joy.

"Yes, I must admit, I didn't think he had it in him," Master Fwap calmly remarked. "But my own master, Fwaz-Shastra Dup, had foreseen that he would solve the riddle. As usual, my root guru was correct."

"Okay, Master Fwap, but what about the riddle, when do I get to that part? And, if you don't mind my asking, I thought you said that you and the Oracle weren't going to come into any of these astral dimensions with me?"

"You've already solved the riddle!" the Oracle shouted.

"The Oracle's correct," Master Fwap calmly responded. "You've done it."

"But what are you guys doing here in the dimensions with me? Did you come in just to tell me that I've done it?"

"We are not in the dimensions with you," Master Fwap said in a soft and even tone of voice, as if he were explaining something complicated to a small child. "We are in the here and now, at my temple in Katmandu."

"Wait a minute, Master Fwap. Aren't our bodies still back in the cave of enlightenment, in the Anapurna Himalayas?"

"No," Master Fwap replied, shaking his head gently from side to side.

"Master Fwap and Master Oracle, are you trying to tell me that we teleported our bodies all the way from the cave of enlightenment back here to Katmandu?"

"Precisely," replied the Oracle, with a tone of proud achievement in his voice.

"But this can't be real. I mean, I don't even know how I did it!"

"You will never know," Master Fwap proceeded to explain. "Your second attention did it, as did ours."

"Master Fwap, I am seriously speechless. Was that the answer to the riddle, being able to teleport back here?" I asked with incredulity.

"Evidently," the Oracle replied, in a flat and suddenly bored tone of voice.

"Listen, my young friend," the Oracle continued. "What your second attention did just now wasn't a very big deal from our point of view. We did something a little more difficult, didn't we, Fwap?"

"We did, indeed," Master Fwap replied, "although, honored

Oracle, you must admit it was relatively easy compared to what our own masters made us do when we were his age, in order to regain our past-life enlightenments."

"Yes," the Oracle sighed, as a far-away look filtered across his eyes, as if he was remembering something from a long-forgotten past.

"Excuse me, but would either of you please tell me what you just did that was so hard?" I had to ask, the suspense was starting to get to me.

"Why, we brought back your snowboard and knapsack with us," replied the Oracle. "See, they are lying right behind you, just turn around and have a look for yourself."

I turned my head around and there they were; both my snowboard and my knapsack were lying on the floor behind me.

"It was harder to bring them back than you might suppose," the Oracle remarked as an afterthought. "But we didn't want you to lose your precious snowboard. You'll need it to take lessons on from your new German friend."

Master Fwap then cracked up completely. Then the Oracle joined him. The two of them laughed and laughed until tears covered their entire faces. Eventually their laughter subsided.

"Well, now what do I do?" I asked in a totally dumbfounded voice.

"I suggest that you return to the hostel for a few days and begin to read the third section of *The Handbook for Enlightenment*. In the meantime, take a few snowboarding lessons from your new German friend, and when you feel the time is correct, you can bring her over and introduce her to us," replied Master Fwap.

"We'll be here when you two arrive," the Oracle said with a smile.

I stood up, picked up my snowboards and knapsack, bowed

to Master Fwap and the Oracle, and walked down the dark temple corridor and out of the front door, into the stark, bright Katmandu morning sunlight.

Walking down the steps from Master Fwap's temple, somehow I just knew that I was at the beginning of what was going to prove to be a very special day.